# HOFFMAN vs. HOFFMAN

*By the same author*

Clint Eastwood, the Man behind the Myth

The Decline and Fall of the Love Goddesses

# Hoffman vs. Hoffman

## *The Actor and the Man*

by
Patrick Agan

ROBERT HALE · LONDON

© Patrick Agan 1986
First published in Great Britain 1986

Robert Hale Limited
Clerkenwell House
Clerkenwell Green
London EC1R OHT

Agan, Patrick
Hoffman vs. Hoffman.
1. Hoffman, Dustin    2. Moving-picture
actors and actresses——United States——
Biography
I. Title
791.43'028'0924    PN2287.H56

ISBN 0-7090-2594-7    CHX-LS

792.092
HOFFMAN

Typeset in Palatino by
Kelly Typesetting Ltd., Bradford-on-Avon, Wiltshire
Printed in Great Britain by St. Edmundsbury Press,
Bury St. Edmunds, Suffolk
Bound by Woolnough Bookbinding, Northants

# Contents

# Illustrations

# Acknowledgements

The author wishes to thank the following people, publications and friends for their varied but important input to this book:

Doug McClelland and the Doug McClelland Collection *The Hollywood Reporter*, and especially Robert Osborne and Hank Grant, for keeping everyone abreast of the news, Radie Harris, Douglas Brode's *The Films of Dustin Hoffman*, *The New York Times*, *The New Jersey Star-Ledger*, Sheila Benson of the *Los Angeles Times*, *American Film*, the late Arthur Bell, *Rolling Stone Magazine*, Cliff Jahr, Diana Maychick, the *New York Post*, *People Magazine*, Bertil Unger, Jeff Lenburg's *Dustin Hoffman–Hollywood's Antihero*, *Focus on Film*, *Films in Review*, Charles Champlin, R. Couri Hay, *Cahiers de Cinema* and William Goldman *for his Adventures in the Screen Trade*. Special thanks to Jo-Ann Geffen & Associates, Nancy Hamilton, Julie Nathanson, Barbara Jo Peterson of the Henri Bollinger Organization, Dick McInnes, Joan Horn, Gerry Turnbull and Patrick Stockstill of the Margaret Herrick Library of the Academy of Motion Picture Arts and Sciences.

# Dedication

This is dedicated to my partner and adviser (not that I've heeded every word!), Dennis Dumont.

And to my patient and faithful agent, Jay Garon, who has been there when I've needed him most.

# Preface

## First Glance

'I'm just an actor, and I don't feel I represent anybody.'

The above is an early quote from Dustin Hoffman, given at the time of fresh movie stardom, a time when people wanted to know what to expect next. Cagily, he circled around the question and, in truth, has continued to do so ever since.

If one insists he must represent someone, the only possible answer is that he magnifies and explores a little bit of all of us in his screen characters, because, after eighteen major films, he still doesn't speak for any*one* in particular. Instead, though he has been a major star since *The Graduate* in 1967, he remains an enigma, a chameleon who purposely changes faces, accents and personalities with every role in order consistently to expose new facets of an enormously complex and strong-willed personality.

'I was very affected by Lee Strasberg when I studied with him; he would say over and over again, "There is no such thing as juvenile or an *ingénue* or a villain or a hero or a leading man. We're all characters." I was maybe twenty-one years old, I'd just come to New York to study, and it hit me very strong because I was a victim of casting.'

Right from the start, Hoffman's five foot six inches height and looks were a handicap in his finding roles. For several years the best acting jobs he got were definitely off-beat as well as Off-Broadway, including that of a crippled German homosexual in *Harry, Noon and Night* and one as a Russian clerk in *Journey of the Fifth Horse*. One can only wonder where his career would have gone if it hadn't been for the sharp eye of director Mike Nichols discerning his potential for *The Graduate*.

As for Dustin himself, it just might not have mattered, as he stated early on that, 'I just want to be a working actor — I'll play anything as long as it's good.' A nice quote when you're just

1

starting out but a hard one to live up to after tasting the heady wine of stardom.

Happily it seems that Dustin Hoffman has a firm head on his shoulders when it comes to success, as it hasn't changed the basic man as much as it's increased his already strong sense of himself and his commitment and responsibility to making that success stretch across fresh acting boundaries. And, despite his looks, Dustin has been able to find new challenges with practically every film he's made, for, unwittingly or not, he has opened up a whole new world to Hollywood casting directors — the world of the *un*beautiful.

It's been written that Nichols had never experienced a movie failure, but considering that heretofore he'd directed only one, that fact was hardly news. Perhaps the biggest news was the fact that Dustin got to be *The Graduate* at all.

Nichols had just finished making Elizabeth Taylor and Richard Burton look their worst (and act their best) in *Who's Afraid of Virginia Woolf* and was then put in the curious position of dealing with Dustin in a part that was originally created for a 'typical' California surf-god, at least six feet tall with blond hair and a body rippling with muscles. In this case Nichols had to make do with average good looks plus getting a performance that would be powerful enough to take the movie-goer's mind off the difference! It was an enormous challenge for them both but one that Nichols committed himself to from the moment he saw Dustin on stage in the 1966 comic hit play *Eh?* at New York's Circle in the Square theatre.

One of the most convincing aspects of Dustin's performance, ironically, was his own well-modulated physique. While not anywhere near six feet tall *or* blond, his trimly muscled, proportioned body was very much the kind a California kid would naturally build up (as indeed the California-born actor had) and lent credence to the story of a mildly sheltered boy who, upon college graduation, suddenly finds himself in the middle of a steamy affiar with the wife of his father's business partner, the infamous 'Mrs Robinson'.* Add to that his falling in love with her daughter, played by a lustrous Katherine Ross, and you have one of the most unforgettable screen love-triangles in history.

* Anne Bancroft played the role of 'Mrs Robinson' after Susan Hayward turned it down, deeming it 'too salty' for her image. In retrospect, it would have done both her career and her image a world of good.

Looking back, it would seem Nichols' label of 'genius' was well earned, certainly with his casting of *The Graduate*, giving the public its brightest new star of the mid-sixties and setting a trend for a new breed of unhandsome leading men that would shortly include Al Pacino, Robert De Niro and others.

Dustin was the last person ever to imagine he'd singlehandedly change the face of the All-American movie hero in *The Graduate*. In fact, for a long time after its overwhelming success he refused to be overwhelmed at all, clinging to anonymity (a quality he values highly) until he finally realized that fame was here to stay and his days of walking the streets of New York unnoticed were over.

Naturally Hollywood, in its usual corporate wisdom, began bombarding the actor with *Graduate*-like scripts with Benjamin Braddock-type parts – he could have made a career out of that role – but Dustin was smart enough to avoid that trap. Said he, succinctly, 'I don't want to be the Andy Hardy of the sixties.' And those few who didn't believe him certainly came around when it was announced he'd star in *Midnight Cowboy*.

'After *The Graduate*, everyone said, "Well, Mike Nichols has got this guy who's just playing himself." I got so upset when I read that, I couldn't wait to prove it wrong, and when I chose to do *Midnight Cowboy* Nichols called me up at one point and said, "Are you sure you want to play Ratso Rizzo? It's not even the star role. You're secondary and it's such an unattractive role [the crippled New York street hustler] and you could kill the career that you established with *The Graduate* – you should play Joe Buck." But I was out to show that I was a character actor – and, in fact, Benjamin was as much a character as any part I had done – and that I was not just this nebbish kid that Nichols found.'

Recently Hoffman has finally admitted that, 'What I really wanted, deep down, was to be a movie star' after *The Graduate*'s success, but at the time it seemed the farthest idea from his mind, with *Midnight Cowboy* seeming perfect proof. As Ratso Rizzo he quickly dispelled any lingering doubts that his was a one-personality talent for he couldn't have found a role more distant and different from Benjamin. Talk about a 180-degree turn! He went from young California rich boy to worn-out New York City street-poor hustler, and the choice proved eminently worthwhile. In 1967 he had been Oscar-nominated as Best Actor for *The Graduate*, and two years later he was nominated again after *Cowboy's* nervously enthusiastic reception.

It was a time for changes in Hollywood's thinking in many ways, and Dustin's timing was absolutely right.

Remember, the mid-sixties were hard times for movie stars. The young and beautiful crop left over from the end of the fifties such as George Hamilton, Susan Kohner, Sandra Dee and Connie Stevens were heading nowhere except the horror-film cycle, while established stars like Elizabeth Taylor and Richard Burton were stretching in every available direction from *Virgina Woolf* to *The Taming of the Shrew* – in fact, they'd stretch in just about any direction offered as long as they got their $ million salaries up front.

There's no question that Liz and Dick were *the* stars of that decade, gambolling about the globe with their assorted pets and children, luggage and hairdressers, not to mention the Press seemingly always on hand to record Elizabeth's latest diamond ring or sable coat. Like glamorous dinosaurs the pair moved inexorably to the days when their popularity extended only as far as the tabloids and no longer to the ticket-buyers. By then, however, they'd amassed such a huge personal fortune that they gave the impression they truly couldn't have cared less.

Most of the mature stars, including Ava Gardner, Gregory Peck, Tony Curtis, Susan Hayward, William Holden and Audrey Hepburn, were gravitating to Europe for film jobs, finding Hollywood suddenly a lonely place. Even perennial hit-makers like Doris Day and Natalie Wood were coming a cropper with pictures such as *Caprice* and *Sex and the Single Girl* respectively.

In short, Hollywood needed a new star attraction, and Dustin Hoffman seemed to be it, complexities, anxieties included.

To describe Hoffman as 'just complex' is similar to describing San Francisco's Golden gate as 'just a bridge', Mount Rushmore as 'just a sculpture' or St Paul's Cathedral as 'just a church'. There's much more going on than can be summed up in one word.

A basic dictionary definition of 'complex' is a) 'a whole made up of complicated or interrelated parts', b) 'a group of repressed desires and memories that exerts a dominating influence upon the personality' and c) 'an exaggerated reaction to a subject or situation'. Broken down into these degrees of definition, 'complex' makes a bit more sense in Dustin's case.

One aspect of his career has been a rampant streak of perfectionism, that has consistently marked his work. Dustin likes it *right*, no matter what it takes, and that quality has only grown and strengthened over the years. And no challenge seems too big for the little man to tackle.

He has also recently shown a quite remarkable ability to personalize a role to fit what is literally happening in his life, as in *Kramer vs. Kramer*. Undergoing a divorce in his personal life, he was willing and able to bring all the hard-won knowledge and pain to his role as Ted Kramer, a hardworking man (*that* Dustin could relate to) who suddenly finds himself a single parent saddled with all the inherent problems, including the wife who eventually wants to claim their child after he's carefully restructured his life (and his son's) without her. Hoffman has played many a poignant part but none had hit home quite like this one because it reflected a portion of his soul that he himself had heretofore never had to deal with: the exposure of an unhappy marriage and the consequences on all concerned.

So convincing was he, though, as Ted Kramer, that he finally won his Best Actor Academy Award. The Academy might not have been used to him enough when he was nominated for *The Graduate* or flexible enough to recognize his versatility as the *Midnight Cowboy*'s friend Ratso, or gutsy enough to accept his compelling portrait of the tragic clown Lenny Bruce in *Lenny* (1974), but in *Kramer vs. Kramer* they finally recognized the combination of actor and man, illusion vs. reality, and he won. There were other awards for *Kramer* and responses on it all from Hoffman, but, remember, this is just a glance, a first one, at his remarkable career.

After two years off screen, Dustin broke yet more new ground in *Tootsie, the* comedy hit of 1983, a mega-hit, as it were, bringing in yet another new adjective into the movie business. As he'd done before, there was a great deal of Dustin's imprint on the final product, the story of an egocentric Broadway actor who is so demanding that no one will work with him. Dustin faced perhaps his ultimate acting challenge as his character of Michael Dorsey, in order to get a job, changes into an actress – Dorothy Michaels – right before our eyes. As Dorothy, he rises to stardom on a soap opera only to fall in love with the show's young star, beautifully played by Jessica Lange (to the point of her winning an Oscar as Best Supporting Actress of 1983).

Critics were lavish in their praise of *Tootsie*, and Dustin was quick to point out that he'd taken a hand in the writing, producing and directing of it. In fact, according to him, the basic premise of the film was his idea, one hatched while walking through Manhattan one day with a friend. He voiced a thought about what it would be like to be a woman. 'I've always wondered how many experiences we miss out on, being men. Is it a radically different experience going through life, depending on what sex you are? Let's see if I could play a man forced to impersonate a woman, then experiencing life from the other point of view.'

That was the seed from which *Tootsie* sprang, making one wonder what Dustin's *next* big idea might be.

While it's impossible to guess what he'll do in the future or just where his career will end up – 'I want to live to be old as Picasso and work till my dying day' – it is time for an evaluation of what he's done and may do at this midpoint in his life. Established at the top as a mega-star, one can only wonder what will be next. But one thing is certain, by glancing back at his past: it won't be boring.

# 1

# An unorthodox debut

'God bless us all, goddamn it!', and with those words Dustin Hoffman began his acting career. He was in the seventh grade at the time and had been chosen for the part of Tiny Tim in a school production of *A Christmas Carol* because he was the shortest kid in his class. (There might have been one just a bit shorter but Dustin said later that he really wanted the part and scrunched down in the line-up of boys and got it,. The 'goddamn it!' part came later as a dare from some fellow students at Los Angeles' John Burroughs Junior High School, a dare that appealed to the twelve-year-old who had already proven himself as less than an enthusiastic student.

In fact, the major reason Dustin was interested in the role was because its rehearsals would get him out of some tedious classes. He got his wish after his pageant performance: he was suspended from school! Even at the age of twelve, Dustin realized he'd have to do things the hard way, to become the class clown in order to gain approval from his peers because he'd been cheated of the basic California dream. Born on 8 August 1937 at LA's Queen of Angels Hospital, the second son of Harry and Lillian Hoffman, that dream was his honest birthright but it passed him by.

Later he admitted: 'I always felt like an intruder in the family. I came six years after it started.' Dustin didn't start talking until he was 3½ year-old but once he learned the gift of the gab, he used it constantly. Mother Lillian once described him as a 'clown from the word "go",' yet that came later, when Dustin was forced to come to grips with the fact that he'd never be tall and he'd never be handsome. Before he turned twelve, the family had moved some six times to various Los Angeles addresses, making Dustin constantly have to prove himself to new friends and, hopefully, new girls.

It must have been a difficult time for the youngster. On one hand he was happy to leave an environment of children who didn't like him and yet having to face another crowd of 'friends', not that different from those he'd left behind, was not much better.

When he was old enough to recognize it, Dustin compared his father's erratic work struggles with those of Willy Loman in *Death of a Salesman*, a realization that stayed with him until he could actualize it years later when he did the play – and played that part – himself. In the meantime, however, Dustin's adolescent sexuality was the main thing on his mind.

'I really don't think you get over anything that had strong early effects on you. In my memory (I realize) I took my feelings about myself off of what girls thought of me and until puberty all the girls thought I was little and cute but when serious stuff like pubic hair and breasts came in I was suddenly out of vogue.'

To compensate, he tried masking his unattractiveness beneath a façade consisting of his wide sense of humour. He really didn't have much of a choice. Instead of hitting the almost obligatory California height of six feet, Dustin stalled at five feet six inches, and instead of the classic chiselled features of the California stereotype male, usually topped by bleach-blonded hair, he had to accept and live with an irregular face dominated by his father's large nose and an unruly mop of black hair. Now there's nothing wrong with that physical combination – that is, in any place other than Southern California – so it's no surprise that his early attention-getting clowning eventually led him to an acting career, one he started in earnest, he says, because he wanted to get to know the kind of pretty girls who'd ignored him in his early youth.

Dustin's quest for his own identity began early. His brother, Ron, some 6½ years older, was the family achiever, an A student and varsity athelete, while Dustin was skinny and short with a case of acne that seemed to last most of his life and a set of braces on his teeth that lasted for eight years of it. 'I was the King of Acne, and the braces were my crown.'

A sickly child, the closest he got to athletics in school was gymnastics, and he had to drop that after doing a back flip on his bed and landing on a chair! After that Dustin took up tennis, but that didn't do much for his school image because, in the fifties, 'tennis was considered pretty much a sissy sport.'

Naturally his peer group was not supportive, saying he looked like a rat with his dark, ever-moving eyes, little body and big nose, which made Dustin feel more the outsider than ever. He once delivered a book report based on Jimmy Durante's biography, *Schnozzola*, and when he talked of Durante's youth and the pain caused him by his oversize nose, tears spilled out of his eyes and he had to leave the room.

Dustin's quest for attention and acceptance began to spawn his *need* to act, and when he finally made the move to do it, it was a revelation. 'Acting was the first time in my life when I felt attractive, the first time I felt as though I knew what I was doing. It was like finding a new family.'

The family he was born into was, in Dustin's mind, never a particularly close one. His father, Harry, had moved West from Chicago in the early thirties with grand hopes of becoming a movie-producer, while his wife prepared herself to be a producer's gorgeous wife, spending time on making herself as attractive as possible so she'd be ready when good fortune hit. Two first-generation American Jews, they had their own dream to follow and worked diligently at finding it and making it come true.

Harry's father had died when he was only nine, so he was a man used to responsibilities and challenges. Twice he'd beaten tuberculosis, and over the years he had developed a tough, upfront attitude of survival. Unfortunately Hollywood proved to be an exceptionally tough nut to crack. One of his first jobs there was digging ditches on the new-born freeway system, and there was even a period of bankruptcy for the family to endure. As for those Hollywood dreams, the closest Harry got to the movie business was when he was hired to supervise props at Columbia Pictures.

Lillian was a perfect partner for him, encouraging him on through the rough years of the Depression and working hard to make an attractive and well-run home for their two sons. A dedicated movie fan, as were so many millions during the thirties, she reportedly went so far as to name her children after favourite stars: Ron for Ronald Colman and Dustin after silent screen idol Dustin Farnum. Later she totally denied this. 'That's just not true,' she exclaimed. 'I'm not even old enough to remember Dustin Farnum!' (Farnum starring in De Mille's *The Squaw Man* in 1913 and worked steadily in films until 1926, so it seems likely she did remember him but coyly chose not to admit it.) As for son Ron, the closest he got to emulating his namesake came in 1939 when, at eight years old, he played a walk-on part in Frank Capra's *Mr*

*Smith Goes to Washington.*

So the bitter-sweet reality of Hollywood was a part of Dustin's life from the beginning, and it was something that he had to absorb over the same years he was also juggling and exploring his personal emotions and talents.

When he was ten, someone gave the Hoffman family an old piano, and Dustin quickly found he had a natural talent for it, yet it was five years before he took it seriously. At fifteen he transferred to Los Angeles High School and started studying piano in earnest. His mother encouraged him, urging him to use his talent to bring more 'culture' into his life, but instead he found himself becoming a fixture at school parties – playing the piano. Dustin also made the tennis team, but it was the piano he hoped to use as a way to a social breakthrough.

Finally, through his music, Dustin gained a measure of popularity, but unfortunately this talent didn't bring the girls flocking to him as he'd hoped. He later recalled how he'd play song after song just waiting for that special girl to come sit alongside him and tell him how gifted he was. One interviewer later suggested he may have seen John Garfield and Joan Crawford's *Humoresque* one time too many!

Besides his tennis, Dustin worked off steam in marathon-running and, as a part-time job, sold newspapers at a stand on Beverly Boulevard, where a shopping centre stands today. He was a busy boy, constantly trying to use up his vast supply of excess engery in what he thought to be productive ways. Cataloguing all these things carefully in his mind, he was later to draw on practically all of them as an actor.

By this time Dustin's father had embarked on a successful career as a furniture-designer, and prosperity at last loomed large for the Hoffmans. After high school Dustin entered Santa Monica City College with a major in music. As was usual for him, he also looked for a few easy credits and signed up for acting courses as well.

All this might have continued serenely had it not been for his mother. Now that her husband was finally tasting success, Lillian felt it was time to expand her own horizons and did so by signing up for some courses at the same college her son was attending. Much younger-looking than her age and extremely attractive, her presence on campus frankly embarrassed her son, particularly when she started getting better grades! At home, Harry was none to happy having his wife seemingly searching for a new lifestyle, and the end result was that they both quit the school. Dustin qualified and entered the Los Angeles Conservatory of Music, expanding his musical studies to include both classical piano and jazz.

In early 1957, after some months of work at the school, Dustin began having doubts about making a career of the piano, and as those doubts grew stronger, so did the memories of the acting classes he'd taken the year before at Santa Monica.

Those classes had made an important mental connection for Dustin in that, for the first time in his life, he'd felt he really *belonged* as part of a close-knit, creative ensemble. Also they had given him the rare opportunity simply to step away and transcend his own personality and imagined physical deficiencies to the point where he later summed up those initial reactions, saying, 'What attracts me [to acting] is the dreamlike way of going through life.' Certainly this was a naïve reaction to his first encounter with what would be his profession, but there were others, primarily the chance to create and work in an art not as isolated as the practising of music. Dustin liked people even if they didn't seem to care much for him, and when it came down to being alone with his piano or among a group of learning actors, he shortly chose the latter. In acting, people would *have* to pay attention to him, have to praise him if he was good and therefore *have* to appreciate him. That he wanted desperately.

Dustin made the decision to be an actor on his own and without much family encouragement.

At the next family Passover dinner at his aunt Pearl's, she asked him what he was going to do with his life. Be an actor, said Dustin. Pause. You can't, said Aunt Pearl. You're not good-looking enough.

Despite that curt opinion, Dustin applied to and was accepted by the prestigious Pasadena Playhouse, an institution whose motto was 'Work with the stars, *become* a star.'

After taking one look at the 'walking surfboards' that peopled the Playhouse, Aunt Pearl's words came ringing back to Dustin and he almost left. If the average streets and schools of Los Angeles depressed him with their parade of golden boys, the students at the Playhouse only compounded his self-doubts. To him they seemed perfect, not a spot on them nor a suntan less than perfect. Since he admittedly was partially attracted to acting so he could meet girls artist-to-artist, he was momentarily at a loss, but happily his true artistic calling to performing won

11

out.

Bypassing the pretty boys, Dustin picked out people more like himself to make friends with, one of whom was a young novice named Gene Hackman. He also chose an anti-Establishment image which set him even further apart from the sun-bronzed mainstream student. 'Dusty wore a tattered sheepskin jacket and played the bongo drums,' says Hackman, who himself stuck it out at the Playhouse for only four months. A short time, true, but long enough for him and Dustin to become – and remain to this day – best friends. While Hackman went off to New York, Dustin stayed at the Playhouse, diligently learning the basics of his new-found craft and slowly coming to the realization that, if he was to succeed, it would be as a character actor and not a leading man.

Despite his personal reservations Dustin slowly began to fit into the general routine. The man who'd become his favourite teacher, Barney Brown, took an interest in him and steered him towards roles that fitted him, most importantly by casting him in a production of Arthur Miller's *A View From the Bridge*. Brown was a stern taskmaster but was quickly won over to the specialness of Dustin's talent. In fact, he told him he had 'something unique' to offer but added, 'You'll probably be thirty before it happens for you.' Obviously, in the light of Dustin's career, the man was either a prophet or a mind-reader because it did take just that long before Dustin Hoffman became a star with *The Graduate*.

The Playhouse opened up a new world for Dustin and as he grew accustomed to it he also grew to realize that, like Hackman, if he was going to make it as a stage actor, that would happen in New York, so he quietly made mental plans to go there. In the meantime he concentrated on his studies and found that despite his looks there were many women at the Playhouse who weren't as unapproachable as he'd first thought. This time, instead of picking classes to avoid work, as he'd done in high school, he picked them because of the present student bodies. Admittedly they were onstage relationships but they served as both a release and a relief. 'I'd be on stage rehearsing a scene, saying to a girl, "I love you, I really care about you," things I'd wanted to say for years to girls. All my life I'd been writing and acting scenes in my mind where I'd be telling guys off and telling girls I loved them; all day long in class, that's what I'd been doing, transferring myself instead of listening. I felt a naked passion for acting; getting laid was the only thing I ever felt that way about —

no, not just getting laid, getting to know a girl and sit in front of a fire with her, and be *loved* and be *accepted.'*

In all, Dustin's two years at the Playhouse were a success, and when he left in 1958, he did so with more self-confidence than he'd ever had before. Now was the time to test it, and with the blood of spunky Harry and Lillian flowing in his veins, he left the familiarity of Los Angeles behind him, much as they had long ago left Chicago, for the mean streets of New York City, taking with him a renewed spirit and his old pal Gene Hackman's telephone number.

# 2

# New York City

Coming of age in New York City.

To any twenty-one-year-old, New York can first appear an awesome, unfriendly and dangerous place, yet to Dustin there was an instant affinity between him and the city that quickly made it his home. Sure aspects of it frightened him, particularly at the beginning before he'd had a chance to find a place for himself there. 'This city is cold and lonely and terrifying,' he admitted. He came to the city with little money, no place to stay and few friends but he also came with firm determination to survive. The young actor who said he came to New York 'because I didn't want to fail at home' soon found that, spiritually at least, New York would be his new one.

Unlike the vast low-rise reaches of Los Angeles, Dustin found himself suddenly a citizen of the canyons of Manhattan. Hackman, then working as a furniture mover to support his young family, nonetheless welcomed Dustin as best he could, letting him sleep on his kitchen floor next to the refrigerator. 'Every night at 2 and 4 a.m. it would have a heart attack. It went "BrrrrrrrrrrrrrRRRRRRR" and woke me up.'

The landscape of the new city was one thing to get used to but the stony ground of the theatre world for a beginner was quite another, and Dustin spent a lot of hours sleeping on Hackman's floor instead of making the merciless rounds of unimpressed acting agents.

While making his way across country, Dustin had worked at various local theatres, including one in Colorado where he at least made friends, but he quickly found that those meagre credits didn't mean much in New York. There were even some days when he slept around the clock to block out what he was sure was a hostile world.

Slowly, though, and with Hackman's encouragement, Dustin began getting familiar with his new surroundings, haunting various museums and theatres and in general getting the feel of his new homebase.

In a city of perpetual newcomers, the world of the theatre attracted even more of these than the rest of New York, a golden magnet for thousands of untried actors all eager for stardom. Before that, however, the smart ones realized they had to be as eager for two other things: a means to survive and an agent. Luckily Dustin had some office skills and was able to get part-time work. 'I was a very good typist. In high school if you got kicked out of class, you were sent to study hall, and if you got kicked out of study hall, you were sent to typing class . . . consequently, I can type eighty words a minute.' Dustin found he hated the confined space and atmosphere of office work, however, and many times simply walked out on jobs by not returning from his lunchbreaks. 'After a while I began to bring my own lunch to work just to stop myself,' he later recollected.

Since Dustin's acting experience was limited, he tried a new scheme to convert his various jobs into acting exercises. When Macy's hired him to sell hockey games in their toy department, he immediately adopted a French-Canadian accent and wore a Montreal Canadian's hockey shirt to help push them. On another ocassion at Macy's, Gene Hackman brought his two-year-old son, Christopher, in to visit, and Dustin set the child up on the counter and jokingly tried to sell him as a life-size doll! One customer actually had her money out before Hackman called a halt. It was getting too realistic for him.

But perhaps the most demanding job Dustin had was as a hospital attendant at the New York Psycho-analytic Institute, where he got to relate to the mad on a very personal level, seeing people in their most emotionally naked states and often losing themselves in their madness and assuming new personalities on a second's notice. As an actor who simulates emotions, he found it fascinating, though disturbing.

Dustin observed the patients with a rapt intensity, almost as if by doing so he'd find out that the secret behind their rapid changes was somehow their own choice. An actor assumes a new personality at will but it became increasingly, and painfully, obvious that these poor souls did so out of an insane necessity to change reality. He also observed the effects of their illness on the loved ones left behind as they wandered strange corridors of the mind, and that was another sobering reality to deal with. Once the wife of a doctor arrived to visit her patient/husband, and

Dustin witnessed the temporary transformation of the stroke-ridden man back into the person he'd been before. In the past the man had not recognized his wife at all, but this day, for a few fleeting seconds, he did, running to her and yelling 'I can't help it – I'm trying' before reverting back to the stranger his illness had made him.

It wasn't long before Dustin became aware of the emotional drawbacks of the job and what its strain was doing to his own pysche. He hated most holding down the patients during shock treatments and eventually had to quit the job after eight months, half-joking, 'I realy enjoyed it until it got to me. I've always been attracted to mental illness. They wanted to commit me, so I quit.'

It was shortly after that, in August 1959, that he got his first New York acting job in Gertrude Stein's *Yes Is For a Very Young Man* at Sarah Lawrence College in Bronxville. The pay wasn't much — 'I paid my own train fair out there, got $30 and ended up with 3' — but it did give him a chance to act and also to meet some of the female students of the prestigious school. Being one of the few males on the campus with a captive audience of a thousand young women was Dustin's idea of a pretty good deal.

As for the money, Lillian and Harry were sending their son $200 a month to help him out, money that in the 1959 economy went quite a way. Sure he had to scramble for odd jobs but his parents generous support was there for at least two years to help smooth the path. Without that support he freely admits 'I wouldn't have made it.'

Also he realized that, after a lifetime of social rejection by his LA peers, he now faced professional rejection in New York. Dustin and his pals Hackman and Robert Duvall were all part of the vanguard of unpretty boys tackling the stage at that time, and all doing it with much trepidation. 'I couldn't make the rounds [of casting offices],' he said 'I couldn't stand the rejection. They were looking for faces, photogenic faces. You had to have a nice face to take a photo. Then you walked in, sat down, and said, "I have the face." If you didn't have the face, you slipped your photo under the door and ran away. I worked and I studied and I cried and I slept a lot.'

Out of town Dustin spent a winter in North Dakota, where, among other things, he directed a production of *Two For the Seesaw*, an experience he relished. In fact, he enjoyed the whole experience so much he considered staying there, but realizing that was basically a cop-out for his real ambitions, he returned to

New York with new credits for his résumé and renewed determination to get into a good drama class.

Buoyed by his out-of-town acceptance, he went right to the top when he sought entrance to Lee Strasberg's Actor's Studio, that goldmine of talent in the fifties which produced and polished a virtual *Who's Who* of the stage, including Paul Newman, George C. Scott, Geraldine Page, Ben Gazarra and Marlon Brando. Unfortunately Strasberg wasn't enthusiastic, and Dustin was rejected by his studio four times in a row. Hackman and Duvall, Strasberg students themselves, had recommended Dustin to Strasberg, and while he liked the California youth's enthusiasm, he deliberately separated his personal feelings until he was finally convinced that Dustin had the talents requisite for membership. On his fifth try, and after much work and soul-searching, Dustin was able to demonstrate that he belonged and was finally accepted.

He immediately went to work to prove to Strasberg that his confidence was not misplaced and applied hmself to learning and living 'The Method' technique of acting advocated by the Actor's Studio, expanding his earlier attempts to 'personalize' his craft by using it in real life, as he'd done before. Taking a job as a waiter in a small restaurant, he'd again affect his French accent when dealing with customers, which worked until one evening a real Frenchman showed up for dinner and wanted to pursue the conversation!

Dealing with the general public was always preferable to Dustin because it gave him that many more people to bounce his personality off. A major chance to do that with a live Broadway audience came when he took a gig as an orange-drink salesman at the Longacre Theatre where the great Zero Mostel was starring in *Rhinoceros*.

Blacklisted from films by the House UnAmerican Activities Committee in the fifties, Mostel, was making a smash hit out of the off-beat comedy, one of the most successful of the 1961 season. After dealing with his customers, Dustin would sneak inside the theatre and observe Mostel and company, studying, comparing acting styles and, in general, absorbing it all for eventual use in his own life and career.

Happily Dustin was able to share his new knowledge and thoughts on acting almost immediately, when he started an acting class at New York's East Harlem Boys' Club. Located on West 110th Street, the club was a local haven of culture for the streetwise children who joined it, and they proved an appreciative audience for Dustin's new insights, lapping them up with the enthusiasm of youth. Dustin also directed the boys in several plays, and while he found them more difficult to handle than his South Dakota actors, he didn't mind. Instead he made their lack of formal training work for them, channelling their energy into new and special interpretations, into a discipline they'd formerly been missing in life. It was a rewarding experience for all concerned.

These were busy months for Dustin, with him bounding between classes to the Boys' Club to the endless string of part-time jobs, which now included stringing Hawaiian leis in a small, sweaty factory, working in the office of the City Morgue and another memorable stint as a waiter. The generous manager of Rudley's restaurant told Dustin he could have free food. Taking him at his word, Dustin proceeded to down six of their thinly sliced steak specials — and then was promptly fired.

Professionally his next stage job was in a one-week showcase revival of Sidney Kingsley's *Dead End*, which featured another struggling newcomer, Bill Macy, later to gain television fame as the husband of 'Maude'. 'We put it on at the 41st Street Theatre,' Dustin recalled, 'and I got an agent out of that.' That was certainly a turning point, for Dustin had been struggling for years with the movie actor's basic dilemma – 'I needed an agent to get a job and I needed a job to get an agent!'

The agent went right to work for his new client too, landing Dustin a one-line role in *A Cook for Mr General*, on Broadway. It starred British actor Bill Travers and was greeted with a dubious set of reviews. Though he was little more than an extra in it, Dustin was deeply disappointed when it closed after only a three-week run. Yet, as Dustin saw it, it was a landmark: he'd wet his feet at last in the waters of Broadway, and work, more than ever before, became his favourite four-letter word.

There was also another avenue of his life that was showing promise because he'd recently met and been dating a lithesome ballerina named Anne Byrne. Born in New York City, Anne had been raised in Chappaqua, New York, where she attended the Horace Greeley School, returning to the city to study ballet. Like Dustin, the graceful brunette — at five feet nine inches some three inches taller than Dustin — had decided early on what she wanted out of life and studied diligently at the Professional Children's School and then at the American School of Ballet. Her first professional appearance was in Montreal with Les Grands Ballets Canadiens, where she stayed and worked for two years before returning home and utilizing her classically trained talents in summer stock productions of musicals like *Bye, Bye, Birdie, Fiorello* and *Blossom Time.*

'I was playing piano, for free, at the Improvisation,' says Dustin. 'She had a date with my room-mate and he brought her there. I said to him, I really like that girl. He said, "Tell you what. Give me a week to score. If I don't score I'll turn her over to you." He didn't like to spend more than a week at it. That was the limit of his patience. He didn't score so he turned her over to me. I started going out with her for a month, then I left for summer stock in Fishkill, New York . . . she went back to the Philadelphia Ballet Company. So we closed up shop.'

Anne indeed went to Philadelphia, where, in 1963, she was chosen as one of the original members of the Pennsylvania Ballet, staying with them as a principal dancer for the next three years. Besides dancing, though, Anne also married financier Winfried Schlote and had a daughter, Karina. 'Next time I saw her,' says Hoffman, 'was four years later. She was married, had a baby, and on her way to a divorce.'

The intervening years had obviously been critical ones for Anne, just as they were busy for Dustin as he carefully laid the foundations of his career. After a season with the theatre Company of Boston, during which he stretched his acting muscles in plays by Pinter, Beckett, Brecht and Sartre (and all for the grand salary of $65 a week!), he returned to New York to play 'Pozzo', the slave-driver, in a Circle in the Square revival of *Waiting for Godot*, transplanted there for one night after its Boston run. The play was directed by Ulu Grosbard and marked the beginning of a close personal and professional friendship that would last over twenty years until the film *Straight Time* in 1978.

Right from the start it was a mutual admiration relationship. Dustin appreciated the opportunity to work with the director in such a prestigious project, and Grosbard was extremely impressed with the results, so much so that he frankly admitted he'd never really understood the role of 'Pozzo' until Dustin played it. It was too bad that the engagement lasted only the one night because theatre legend has it that it was a timeless and extraordinary performance, certainly good enough to garner Dustin a lot of New York attention.

When Grosbard shortly began casting the first New York

19

revival of Arthur Miller's *A View From the Bridge* in ten years, he thought of Dustin. Naturally Dustin was familiar with the play from having starred in it years before at the Pasadena Playhouse but, to his initial dismay, Grosbard wasn't looking for an actor. Instead he wanted Dustin as his assistant director and stage manager for the production, which, ironically, was set to star Robert Duvall. Dustin took the job, and it proved a very positive move in the long run. Though disappointed at not acting in the show, he did begin a friendship with one of its young stars, Jon Voight, not to mention getting to spend some time with the playwright himself, Miller.

The celebrated writer was very interested in this revival of one of his major works and often visited the theatre during rehearsals. One day Grosbard took him aside and told him there was a member of the company who would be perfect in the lead role of another Miller masterpiece, *Death of a Salesman*. Miller looked around at Duvall, Voight and others in the cast and then realized Grosbard was pointing just offstage at Hoffman. Miller recalled him as being short and unprepossessing and looking 'as if he had barely gotten out of high school'. Little did either realize that almost twenty years later Dustin would indeed star in *Salesman* on Broadway and to ecstatic reviews. Despite their later falling out, Grosbard obviously did recognize Dustin's talent.

As for the *Bridge* revival, it didn't add any acting credits to Dustin's résumé but it did give him a good long job. The production ran some 780 performances, but Dustin wasn't there on closing night for, by then, he'd auditioned and won the lead in an original Off-Broadway play, *Harry, Noon and Night*.

Its director, George Morrison, thought Dustin's audition 'was the most brilliant I've ever seen', and once into rehearsals he evinced an uncanny ability to submerge his own personality into that of his character, in this case a hunchbacked German homosexual with a limp. As Dustin had done in so many part-time jobs, he literally changed himself into the character, kneading and developing it over rehearsal weeks to the point that when the play opened its director was even more surprised. 'One day he [Dustin] just disappeared before my eyes,' leaving behind a highly tuned character that surprised everyone.

Morrison was delighted, likening Dustin's response to the material to other unions of talent and playwright such as Paul Newman and Tennessee Williams in *Cat On a Hot Tin Roof*, and Geraldine Page in William's *Summer and Smoke*. Little did he know that he was encouraging a pattern of character-exploration that would ultimately sear the nerves of many of Dustin's future directors. Had he known, Morrison might have undermined what would turn into an expensive habit.

Despite the in-house enthusiasm and some good reviews, though, the play was a three-week wonder (read 'flop') and Dustin was out of work again – only this time it was only briefly. As a result of the play he went up for his first television part and got it, playing a crook in an episode of * *The Defenders* which was shown in early April 1965.

Bob Duvall was also cast in the show, so Dustin had the pleasure of working with his friend as well as of exploring a brand new medium, television, and pocketing a check for $500, the most money he'd ever made at one time as an actor. For Dustin the whole thing was a revelation. After his years of stage apprenticeship and training, he was suddenly in front of a *camera* and in the middle of an atmosphere he'd always carefully distrusted: a soundstage. After all, his father hadn't been able to get very far even behind the camera, while his older brother, the 'star' of the family, had managed only one bit part in a long-ago movie. Now here was Dustin getting paid more than he'd ever received before and in a venue of acting alien, and then unwelcome, to him. He approached it as a fluke and, instead of following up by looking for more television work, looked to return to the one-on-one atmosphere of the stage. His determination almost proved fatal.

At the time one of the most successful plays on Broadway was Frank D. Gilroy's Pulitzer Prize-winning drama of an Irish family, *The Subject Was Roses*. It was such a successful production that the original cast, which included Jack Albertson, Irene Dailey and Martin Sheen, was being shipped west for the Los Angeles production, leaving the New York roles up for grabs. Dustin had been seen and admired by Gilroy and was hired as Sheen's understudy, being groomed to take over the role when the original cast's West Coast move was settled. Dustin was delighted at finally having a real part on Broadway, even if it had been originated by another actor.

After the first day's rehearsal he decided to celebrate with a

---

* Other sources identify Dustin's television debut as being in *Naked City*, but that series went off the air in 1963.

girlfriend and offered to make dinner for them at her apartment. After stopping for wine and groceries, he side-stepped to the butcher's for some cubed beef. At the apartment he started up the fondue pot but in his enthusiasm didn't calculate just how quickly the oil would start to sizzle. When he tossed the beef into the hot oil, it exploded out of the pot, splashing over his arms and starting a kitchen fire. Ignoring his scalded arms, Dustin put out the small fire with his hands, severely burning them in the process. Once that was out, the seriousness of his wounds was apparent, sending his friend across the hall to the apartment of a young doctor. After looking at Dustin's burns, he declared them to be third-degree and advised the actor to get to a hospital as soon as possible.

Dustin wanted no part of that, however, as he didn't want to take a chance on losing the role he'd worked so long for. Abusing the theatre adage that 'the show must go on', he turned up at rehearsals the following day 'figuring that I could go on' and disguising his injuries with a long-sleeved shirt. He was determined not to lose this break.

And for one unbelievable week he pulled it off by immersing his own physical pain in the emotional ones of his character, the actor dominating the feelings of the man. Unknown to him, though, was the fact that while he was working/avoiding his situation through, a serious infection was gradually poisoning his bloodstream. Finally he collapsed and was hospitalized, waking up to find himself confronted by a doctor who told him his condition was quite possibly fatal. Now this was a drama Dustin had never encountered before, indeed the ultimate one as he faced death for the first time, and it was awesome. His reactions to this helped shape his later attitudes towards life and death in general. The old story that any hospital veteran will tell you is that, after facing the worst, one is somehow renewed to commit to the future with unused energy, and to a degree Dustin did this, yet his realization was leavened by life's basic message that there are just certain things that one is not in control of. As with his looks and height, Dustin knew there were other unchangeables he'd have to live with.

His illness stabilized finally but upon leaving the hospital he needed a long convalescence of four weeks on doctor's orders, time which necessarily cost him his part. The producers of *The Subject Was Roses* had to recast, but Dustin didn't know this until he returned to the theatre afterwards, hands still lightly wrapped in gauze bandages, only to be told that Walter McGinn, the actor who was to have been *his* understudy, now had the role. The combined trauma of the accident and its consequences closed in on Dustin, and frankly it left the actor in tears. The playwright, Gilroy, understandably sympathetic towards his situation, went to Dustin and explained how time and money had taken the matter out of emotional territory and into the purely practical, a lesson Dustin would remember. There would come a time when he would almost perversely make producers spend their money on movie retakes of his scenes, but the then-and-there of it came when Gilroy asked Dustin if he would become *McGinn's* understudy! It's true that Dustin should have been more upfront about how long his recuperation would take but he wasn't ready for this. He felt betrayed, turning down Gilroy's offer and leaving the theatre in a rage. And instead of a possible year's run in a Broadway hit, he could only look back on that first — and last — day of rehearsal.

Dustin was bitter. His career seemed destined to stall and stall again and he was greatly frustrated by it all. He was determined to make the most of his next role and was quickly signed, again after a brilliant audition, for an Off-Broadway show, *Sergeant Musgrove's Dance*, only to be fired from it within a week.

Once into rehearsals Dustin vented his accumulated frustration by constantly experimenting with his part, taking direction and then enlarging and changing it, to the utter dismay of the director himself. After a few days, the situation exploded. The director decided he didn't need an ego like Dustin's and dropped him from the production.

Dustin was angry at the director but angrier at himself and reached the decision that he needed professional help, entering into analysis that would continue for years – 'I couldn't control myself . . . I kept losing jobs.' The analysis helped him work through his anguish and to temper his ego to the point that, when he heard of auditions for another play by Ronald Ribman, he felt ready to try for it.

*The Journey of the Fifth Horse* was a drama set in nineteenth-century Russia, and Dustin won the role of Zoditch, a publishing clerk who gets the job of deciphering the stolen memoirs of a dying landowner. As usual, he'd given a superb audition for director Larry Arrick, but this director, too, quickly became disenchanted when he began feeling Dustin wasn't 'giving enough of himself at rehearsals.' Quite a switch from

Dustin's last aborted job where he was giving too much! Where is the character, demanded Arrick, to which Dustin replied 'I haven't *found* him yet.' Happily Dustin gradually did find his character's nuances, and the opening night, 22 April 1966, proved electrifying.

Using a high-pitched, nasally projected voice, Dustin walked onstage at the American Place Theatre and went into a performace that had the audience captured. And, for the first time in his career, critics were taking him seriously. They may have carped that the play itself was too loose and imaginative for its origins (Turgenev's *Diary of a Superfluous Man*), but for Dustin's Zoditch there were only superlatives, capped by the *New York Times*' Stanley Kauffmann's opinion that he 'has the vitality of the born actor and the fine control of a skilful one. With sharp comedy techniques, he makes this unattractive man both funny and pathetic . . . Perhaps – the insanities of the theatre world permitting – we will be allowed to watch an extraordinary career develop.'

Dustin felt vindicated at last, and the fact that he was an actor worthy of respect was stamped and certified when he won the 1966 'Obie' Award for Best Actor – Off-Broadway's equivalent to the 'Tony'. Another review underscored his technique when *Esquire* magazine came out saying he was 'an inner directed actor who had to find his character when it came to him'.

At last Dustin had a moment to soak in the warm waters of both good reviews and the knowledge that he'd won them on his own terms, his director's initial qualms be damned. This time both the actor and the man were satisfied but, again, more ground was laid fallow for his ego to grow in.

It was a heady feeling and Dustin enjoyed it, especially the results. When the play shortly closed, his reviews helped him land another great character part in a transplanted Britsh comedy, *Eh?*, which opened at his old stomping ground, the Circle in the Square Theatre, in mid-October 1966.

The production that opened was directed by Alan Arkin, a talent closely attuned to Dustin in that he specialized in the same kind of off-beat humour and parts that Dustin had been playing. And that certainly helped both of them, since Arkin was the third director hired, the other two having quit over 'creative differences' with Dustin, the play's nominal star. Arkin was having none of that, however, and called Dustin down in front of the entire cast on his first day to show exactly who was the boss.

24

Arkin seemed to have an innate understanding of Dustin, later stating, 'There are two kinds of difficult people in the theatre – those who are passionate about their work, and those who are passionate about themselves.' Arkin recognized Dustin as one of the former and, while not indulging him, did let him find the character of the machine-operator, Valentine Brose, on his own and to grow into it naturally. Once again, that was to the delight of the critics: Arkin summed it up by saying, 'There's a point in rehearsal where you want to be a child and pour a glass of water on the rug [just] to see what it's going to look like. Some directors panic. They think the rug's going to look like that on opening night. The director's job should be to open the actor up and, for God's sake, leave him *alone!*' Which, in light of those glowing reviews, was just what Arkin did.

One critic called his performance 'a cross between Ringo Starr and Buster Keaton', going on to compare his antics as the frazzled dye-factory worker in the farce to those of Charlie Chaplin in *Modern Times*. Arkin was as happy about Dustin's success as Brose as the actor himself, concluding, 'I found it a marvellously happy situation. I think we pulled it out of the hat.' The *New York Times* had said that Dustin carried the show and should be seen. And he certainly was.

Almost immediately he got his first movie role – a forty-five-second bit part in *The Tiger Makes Out*. The film was a fleshed-out version of Murray Schisgal's one-act play. *The Tiger*, about a sexually repressed New York mailman, played by Eli Wallach, who attempts to kidnap a 'sexy swinger' only to end up capturing Anne Jackson, a socially repressed Long Island housewife!

Filmed on location in New York City, the comedy was produced by its two stars, Wallach and Jackson, as a sort of revenge against Hollywood. The pair had previously starred in Schisgal's Broadway hit *Luv*, only to lose the movie roles and see them squandered on Jack Lemmon and Elaine May in a tepid production. This Schisgal they all wanted to see done correctly.

The pair began on a shoestring budget of $700,000 but between them and Schisgal they were able to round up a million dollars worth of Broadway talent for cameo appearances by casting their friends. These included masterful character actors such as Elizabeth Wilson, Jack Burns, Charles Nelson Reilly, Sudie Bond and Dustin. He and Schisgal had met earlier in '66 while doing stock theatre in Massachusatts, and it was the beginning of a

25

long and firm friendship. The large, outgoing playwright and the shy young actor with the large nose complemented each other by their senses of humour and an ability to look at the world a little cockeyed but not lose hope. Ultimately it was the pair, wandering through New York one afternoon, who would concoct *Tootsie*.

In *Tiger*, Dustin's part consisted of only one scene, where he's breaking up with his girl friend before she wanders off to be almost grabbed by the preying Wallach. He was very happy to do it as he'd been rethinking his position about film work and had decided that, if he got the chance, he'd do more of it. Flush from his triumph in *Eh?*, he didn't even care that he was to be billed nineteenth in the cast.

One of the people very interested in that stage triumph was Mike Nichols, then looking at actors for his follow-up movie project to *Who's Afraid of Virginia Woolf?*, a youth comedy called *The Graduate*. For Nichols it was an intensely personal challenge meant to prove that his first screen directorial assignment, *Woolf*, had not been a fluke. For that reason he was looking at *everybody* for this new film.

Based on the novel by Charles Webb, *The Graduate* was seemingly a story that cried out for a quite young, quite tall and quite California golden boy — the antithesis of Dustin — but in Nichols' heart one can only wonder if he wasn't looking for an even bigger challenge. After all, he'd just made Elizabeth Taylor look bad, so why couldn't he make an actor like Dustin Hoffman look good? Something to think about as he sat back and watched him romp around the stage in *Eh?*.

After seeing the play, Nichols sent out feelers about the actor, while Dustin, knowing little of the project except that he thought himself totally wrong for it, signed to make a picture in Italy, a 'comedy-thriller' entitled *Madigan's Millions* (originally titled *Un Dollaro per Sette Vigliacchi*). The movie offer was an exciting prospect for the twenty-nine-year-old, promising a glamorous adventure abroad complete with star billing on the finished product and some much-needed hard cash. The amount was only $5,000, but to Dustin that was big money. The film also helped heal Dustin's disappointment at losing the lead role in the upcoming Broadway comedy *The Apple Tree* to Alan Alda.

Certainly the film was no match for a solid Broadway show but it did give Dustin a taste of the international film world of the time. Shot on a small budget in Rome, it was to have starred

George Raft, but failing health forced him to bow out. Cesar Romero took over as Madigan. As 'Jason Fister', Dustin plays a bumbling undercover Treasury agent sent to Italy to locate gangster Madigan's ill-gotten millions, thereby embroiling himself in a series of slapstick mishaps. The whole thing was quickly made – and looks it – and did no one in the cast any real good, though Dustin did get to see Rome, not to metion also getting to know his female co-star, Italian sexpot Elsa Martinelli.

When the movie finally opened in New York (*after* Dustin's enormous success in *The Graduate*), it was quickly dismissed by the critics, one of whom pointed out that, had Mike Nichols seen it before casting Dustin as Benjamin Braddock, he might well have never got his chance to become a star! Producer Joseph F. Levine heard about the picture during the shooting of *The Graduate* and offered to buy up every print of it to save Dustin from embarrassment. * Seen today, it's a curiosity piece at best.

At the time, though, Dustin couldn't have cared less. He had his $5,000 and also got to go back to rejoin *Eh?* in New York, the place where he was finally coming into his own as both an actor and a man.

All his friends, particularly Bob Duvall, were amazed at how his New York learned sophistication had proved to be attractive to women. To Dustin's eternal relief he was becoming a hit with the ladies at last. His unconventional looks, made more attractive by the 1967 styles of long hair and flamboyant clothes, coupled with his mischievous sense of humour and totally honest appreciation of women, had them, suddenly, flocking to him. Remarked Duvall, 'He had more girls than [Joe] Namath', to which his buddy replied, 'There is some fun in knowing you can get away with murder looking quite average.' Dustin was especially attracted to 'long-legged, intelligent, artistically ambitious women,' another friend recalled, all of which made him delightedly susceptible when Anne Byrne returned to New York and they renewed their aborted friendship.

---

* This film has become known as 'Dustin's Folly', the dark skeleton in his professional closet, rattling enough on *The Late Show* to haunt its star. To cement its place in his personal Hall of Horror, critics are quoted as describing the plot as 'moving from engaging to preposterous to ludicrous to unintelligible', while Dustin's portrayal is dismissed with '[He] plays his part like an occidental version of Carlie Chan's Number One Son.'

When they ran into each other in a Greenwich Village laundromat, her first reaction to the tousled-haired actor was that he looked like a slob, 'But I thought he was very sexy.'

While Dustin had been slowly building his career in New York, Anne's life had been equally busy. A true product of her upper-middle-class background in Westchester County, Anne's teenage desires to be a ballerina had necessarily separated her from her peers. 'It was understood that women dated, went to college and married. My dates used to ask me why I was always hanging out with faggots.' So much for artistic appreciation in Westchester!

Anne had persevered, though, and chalked up engagements with several prestigious companies including the Frankfurt Ballet, the New Jersey Ballet and Les Ballets Canadiens and also found time to marry her Philadelphia financier, become the mother of their daughter, Karina, divorce her husband and then leave the Pennsylvania Ballet to return to New York to fulfil a dancer's dream – working under George Balanchine at the New York City Ballet. Like Dustin, Anne had covered quite a lot of territory in a short time, and when they came together again it seemed that both careers were heading into a higher gear.

For Anne, though, her dream of New York dance stardom turned sour, as within a year of her return she left the ballet company to work as a counsellor at both the Lighthouse for the Blind and the Jewish Guild for the blind – certainly worthy and useful places for her to work but still a far cry from the lights of Lincoln Center. Happily she did continue her relationship with Dustin and it was probably the most solid thing in her life. Though some three inches taller than him, she was his ideal woman, his 'shiksa goddess' and he liked it that way. To the short and homely Jewish man, this lanky beautiful Gentile woman was perfection. Intellectually Anne appreciated his needs for privacy and independence and tried to uncomplicate his life as much as she could. In turn Dustin became increasingly devoted to Karina, and a three-year love affair began.

Dustin, at thirty, was at a point where he was finally beginning to appreciate the attentions of one good woman over the hasty affections of many. Turning thirty helped him realize that he'd served his emotional apprenticeship with women just as he'd done professionally with his career, and now was the time for a pay-off.

# 3

# Off-Broadway to movie stardom

While Mike Nichols was still interviewing young hopefuls for *The Graduate*, his interest in Dustin remained, leading him downtown to catch one of his eight-per-week performances in *Eh?* a second time. He came away more intrigued than when he'd seen it the first time. Dustin, returning from his Italian movie experience knowing full well it wasn't *Gone With The Wind*, had come back to the play with a vengeance, improving on what many critics had already called a perfect characterization. The London Times even wrote it up, hailing him as 'the finest new American actor', an opinion obviously reached by many when he shortly went on to win *three* awards for his performance, the Drama Desk Award, the Vernon Rice and the Theatre World. With those in his pocket, Dustin seemed assured of having a long, rewarding and steady career as a stage character star, which was what he'd once said was all he ever wanted from the start. However, that was not the course his career would take, for instead of becoming a Broadway staple, he became a movie idol instead.

At the beginning, both Nichols and producer Lawrence Turman were going to cast their lead character, Benjamin Braddock, to type – a tall and sun-bronzed twenty-year-old, a 'younger' Robert Redford. True, in California, there were thousands of young men who could fill that bill, and, as someone recently quipped, if you threw a frisbee on Malibu Beach, you'd hit half a dozen 'new Redfords', but after seeing Hoffman onstage again, both Nichols and Turman became convinced that it might be more interesting and certainly more of a challenge to cast against the 'walking surfboard' kind of guy that Dustin, in his youth, had always envied.

The call went out to Dustin's agent, and arrangements were made to fly the actor back to his hometown for a screen test. Dustin agreed but he was still wracked with doubts about

29

himself, despite Nichols' enthusiasm.

Katherine Ross had already been set for the pivotal role of Elaine Robinson and, meticulous as usual, Nichols was having her screen test with the candidates for Benjamin in a ten-minute scene from the script. The chemistry between those two actors had to be just right. Ross, then rising up the starlet ranks via films such as *Shenandoah* ('65), *Mr Buddwing* ('66) and the highly regarded *Games* in 1967, wasn't particularly impressed when she first laid eyes on this latest of candidates. 'Here was this little guy, white as a sheet, and he kept saying, "I don't know why I came here. I don't want to do this. I want to go back to character parts".'

The test involved a love scene with Ross, who was, by the way, exactly the kind of girl who'd constantly rejected him in his own California youth, and that made him more anxious than ever. He later remembered, 'I was so nervous and fatigued that I couldn't concentrate. I blew lines repeatedly and did a terrible job, and I knew I wouldn't get the part.' Ross, after testing with a long line of gorgeous blond eager-beaver types, couldn't have agreed more. 'He looked about three feet tall, so dead serious, so humourless, so unkempt, I thought the screen test was going to be a disaster.' And it almost disintegrated into one when, during the test scene, Dustin impulsively reached out and grabbed Katherine's behind. She snapped back at him (after all, this wasn't in the script), making Dustin react to *her* reaction in exactly the same quirky, self-consciously nervous manner that Benjamin Braddock would do. Nichols looked at the test and recognized that Dustin's personalized blend of sexual and emotional confusion was just what he was looking for, and he realized he'd found his star.

Dustin, however, had no clue of Nichols'reaction and returned to New York under a cloud of self-inflicted gloom and despair. Again he took refuge in his Broadway part, feeling convinced he'd failed miserably. 'I never expected [to get] that part. Besides a very bad screen test – I mean I barely had time to study the lines and they fell all over the place – I didn't look the part . . . Without Mike Nichols it wouldn't have happened.' And on his part, Nichols did have a few initial reservations. 'It didn't seem good when we were making it. He didn't know his lines terribly well, and he was nervous. But it was good on film. It was special – he made us laugh.' And making Nichols laugh was no mean feat, considering his own reputation as a comedian, but he appreciated Dustin's vitality plus the fact that, 'He appeared to be simply living his life without pretending.'

Dustin was formally offered the part for, to him, the staggering sum of $17,000, but one wonders if he really believed it until he had the input of another actor whose work he greatly admired.

Often when Dustin was wending his way home over New York's West 11th Street, he'd bump into Mel Brooks. They'd struck up an acquaintance, a kind of 'Hi how are you? OK, are you?' sort of thing which ripened when Brooks, after seeing Dustin work, began chatting about the film he was preparing, *The Producers*. The pair talked seriously of Dustin's playing the role of the crazy Nazi playwright – a part Dustin thought was distinctly right for himself. Once he was chosen for *The Graduate*, however, their idea had to be forgotten, although Brooks was quick to quip that, 'At least you'll get to meet my wife. She's going to seduce you in it.'

And she did with a vengeance.

If *The Graduate* would prove to be the major turning point in Dustin's career, it was of almost equal importance to Mrs Brooks, Anne Bancroft. After her 1963 Academy Award-winning role in *The Miracle Worker*, she had two critical successes with *The Pumpkin Eater* in 1964 (for which she won the British Film Academy Award) and *The Slender Thread* the following year. They weren't hits at the box office, though, and she found herself next substituting for an ailing Patricia Neal in the lurid – and also unpopular – *Seven Women*. Anne badly wanted the part of the soon-to-be-infamous Mrs Robinson and made it clear to its producers that she was available.

Initially Nichols wanted Susan Hayward for the part but after she turned it down his next choice was French actress Jeanne Moreau. After some thought, he realized that she might lend too much of a European quality to what was basically an American story and realized that Bancroft would fill the bill perfectly.

Realizing he had been cast against type, Dustin worried and sweated. 'Even when I was told I had won the role. I agreed to do it only because of my respect for Nichols as a director.' Nichols was smart enough to recognize that and make it work for him, carefully shepherding Dustin through the first days of shooting and helping him adjust to this new environment. And coming from the camaraderie of the theatre world there were adjustments to be made. Dustin told an interviewer that what bothered him most was Hollywood's caste system. 'You walk into these shrouded studio temples, and nobody talks to the crew, and the extras are treated like scum. [As the star] I got called "Sir" so many times I felt as though I were a Kentucky colonel.'

Despite his enthusiasm for Dustin and the rest of the cast, Mike Nichols wasn't the easiest director to work for. Determined to make the film a success, he often overlooked stroking his actors' egos. Dustin recalled that, 'I never had the feeling he was happy with what I was doing . . . he would ocassionally throw out a cookie, but I always felt like a disappointment.'

Sometimes Nichols resorted to outright intimidation to get what he wanted in a scene. Once he took Dustin aside and whispered to him that, 'This is the only day we're ever going to shoot this scene, and no matter how exhausted or lousy you feel, I want you to remember that what you give me is going to be on celluloid for people to see forever and ever. I know you're tired, but when you go to see this film, if you don't like your work in this scene, just remember always that this was the day you screwed up.' To Dustin those words were shattering. For an actor who'd lost several parts because of a lack of satisfying his director *on the spot*, he was first frightened, but then he channelled those feelings into a challenge. He performed the scene perfectly, and from then on the film progressed as smoothly as possible considering the egos involved.

*The Graduate* is basically the story of a boy's sexual passage from adolescence to adulthood, accomplished over one very uneasy summer after his graduation from college.

Benjamin Braddock comes home to his wealthy California parents who promptly throw a party to celebrate and also to begin instilling in him various ideas for his future. One guest, however, has other things on her mind besides Benjamin's career, and that is the wife of his father's business partner, Mrs Robinson. After manoeuvring him into driving her home, she attempts to seduce him in a scene that's one of the comic highlights of the picture. Later, when they meet at a hotel, she completes the job after much bungling, astonishment and embarrassment on his part. Their ensuing affair is further complicated by the arrival home of her daughter, Elaine, and Ben's attraction to her.

Understandably Mrs Robinson fights this new relationship tooth and nail, finally threatening to tell her daughter about her affair with Benjamin in order to break them up. Ben beats her to it, though, only to find Elaine horrified at his confession. She goes back to college a sadly disillusioned girl but Ben follows, trying to convince her of his sincerity. Not believing him, she agrees to marry her old boyfriend. When Ben hears of this, he literally storms the church to stop her, and when Elaine sees him, she realizes she still loves him and rushes to him. The pair run out of the church and get on a bus – she still in her wedding gown – and they head off for what looks to be an uncertain future.

When the film was released in December 1967, it caused an immediate sensation at the box office, buttressed by almost unanimously rave reviews. Critics deemed it a landmark film, capturing the essence of the confusion and self-doubts plaguing so many young people in the sixties. The *New York Times'* Bosley Crowther said it was 'not only one of the best [movies] of the year, but also one of the best seriocomic social satires we've had from Hollywood since Preston Sturges was making them', while the *Saturday Review's* Hollis Alpert claimed it to be 'the freshest, funniest, and most touching film of the year', adding 'The American film may never be quite the same again.' And those two reviews from two of the toughest movie critics were only the tip of the iceberg.

Brendan Gill of the *New Yorker* dubbed it 'one of the liveliest gifts for the season', while the *New Republic* said the film 'gives some substance to the contention that American films are coming of age'.

Dustin's personal reviews from these and other critics were also outstanding. Hollis Alpert stated, 'Dustin Hoffman is the most delightful film hero of our generation. Slightly undersized, totally unsmiling, he stares his way through a series of horrendous, harrowing experiences.' The *New Yorker's* Gill enthused that Dustin 'makes a sensationally attractive movie debut as the troubled hero', while the *New Republic's* Stanley Kauffmann hailed him loud and clear: 'Hoffman, a young actor already known in the theatre as an exceptional talent, here increases his reputation.' An understatement if ever there was one.

Overnight Dustin was a sensation, his face plastered through *Time* Magazine and his talent hailed as not only 'sensational' but 'original' as well, for with Benjamin Braddock he gave birth to a new category of leading man. *Time's* story also labelled him 'a symbol of youth'.

It was all quite overwhelming to Dustin, especially when he

33

quietly returned to his small apartment in New York and his girl-friend, Anne Byrne. The long days of anonymity were over, especially when young female fans tracked down his address and laid siege to his building. It all made Dustin pause and wonder. 'I was doing pretty well off Broadway before *The Graduate* came along. I won an Obie, you know. Well, this sudden stardom stuff completely knocks you out of prespective. If I pass a group of people on the street, I can usually count three before I hear it – "Eeeeee!".'

But if Dustin was taken aback by his sudden success, his parents were thrilled. After their years of subsidizing their son- – now 'My son, the Movie Star', they were now thoroughly enjoying his fame. (Once, during a visit to *The Graduate* set, Harry Hoffman even offered Mike Nichols a piece of directorial advice!) They subscribed to the movie industry trade papers and began charting *The Graduate*'s grosses as they climbed upwards towards an eventual $40 million. Harry would often call his son in New York to tell him how much money the film was making in various cities, while his mother, Lillian, phoned local Los Angeles theatres to see how long the ticket lines were. Many nights she didn't sleep well until knowing just how long.

Meanwhile, back in Greenwich Village Dustin's apartment house was rapidly becoming a fortress. His landlady did her best to help ensure his privacy by taking his name off the mailbox, and while she was changing that from 'Hoffman' to 'Occupant', he was changing his phone number to 'unlisted'.

The Press was dubbing him the screen's new 'anti-hero', an opinion he argued with. True, he certainly thought himself more a character actor than a matinée idol but to open up a whole new category of actor was something else again. 'Wasn't Bogart, even Tracy, off the conventional line for their time? Isn't the anti-hero simply the alienated man?' he followed that comment with his wish of someday playing Holden Caulfield in a movie version of the classic *Catcher in the Rye* and then doubletracked to note of his recent success, 'Johnny Carson rejected me [as a guest]. he thought I was too normal.'

When he saw his name for the first time in block letters on the marquee of a Third Avenue movie house, Dustin projected thoughts of his own mortality, a subject constantly interesting to him, by remarking to an interviewer that, 'It was like death – with my children already grown up, tired of watching my movies at my own request, with my ex-wife at my side and my faithful dog.' That was rather an extraordinary interpretation of his new celebrity, projecting it over all those years and imagined personal changes. To juggle all these conflicting reactions, Dustin set up a new regime. He depended on analysis to help him understand the inward changes he was going through while outwardly he began strenuous work-outs to improve his physique, took ballet lessons to improve his often gangling demeanour and even took singing lessons to hone a talent that might be of possible use later on. Since he'd been dubbed a symbol of an entire generation, he felt obliged to be prepared to symbolize any part of it that producers might require. It was also a great way to work off nervous energy, since his Village walks with Anne on his arm were now curtailed by his new-found fame.

With undeniable public approval, it was logical that he turned more and more to Anne, but he was still not ready to make a permanent commitment. His $17,000 from *The Graduate* was not enough to ensure any real security for himself, let alone her and her daughter. In fact, when all the old bills and friends were paid off, that money was quickly spent and he found himself on the unemployment line, waiting his turn to collect his $55 per week. Admitting that heretofore he'd never made more than $3,000 a year as an actor, and 'If my parents hadn't sent me money every week, I couldn't have survived', he suddenly found himself in a quandary that's happened to others before and since: overnight stardom and no money to back it up.

To top it all off, *The Graduate* was nominated for a total of *seven* Academy Awards: Best Picture, Best Actress for Anne Bancroft's Mrs Robinson, the hit she was so looking for, Best Supporting Actress for Katherine Ross's Elaine, Best Director for Nichols' meticulous guidance, Best Writing, Best Cinematography – and Best Actor for Dustin's Ben Braddock. Besides being the top money-making film of the year, it also looked to be the most honoured. And all of this with the Best Actor nominee being caught on the unemployment line by a *Life* magazine photographer!

Because of the assassination of Martin Luther King on 8 April 1968, the awards were postponed two days, adding to what was already almost unbearable suspense for Dustin, not to mention the rest of *The Graduate* nominees. 10 April, however, was not fated to be a night of great rejoicing, as out of the seven nominations only Mike Nichols walked away with the golden statue, as Best Director. Anne Bancroft had her hit movie and a revived career but what would have been her second Oscar went instead to Katherine Hepburn for *Guess Who's Coming to Dinner*, while the Best Picture nod went to *In the Heat of the Night*. *Bonnie and Clyde*'s Estelle Parsons won over Katherine Ross for Best Supporting Actress, and *Dr Doolittle* won the Cinematography award.

As for Dustin, his competition was formidable, up against Warren Beatty (*Bonnie and Clyde*), Paul Newman (*Cool Hand Luke*), Spencer Tracy (*Guess Who's Coming to Dinner*) and Rod Steiger (*In The Heat of the Night*), yet with the avalanche of great reviews and box-office popularity he thought he had a strong chance to win. Instead it went to Steiger.

Though deeply disappointed, Dustin masked it in interviews, saying that if he'd won he might well have fallen into the trap of over-exposure and typecasting, two things he particluarly wanted to avoid.

Yet Dustin's small amount of available cash made it necessary to think about what would come next workwise. Not that offers didn't start coming in from unexpected sources. 'Wham! All of a sudden you're on everyone's brain. You're offered everything. A clothing company (Petrocelli Suits) want to give me $2,000 in clothes. Me, a stump of a man and they wanted to make me Cesar Romero. I said no.' It was tempting to be offered these movie-star perks but he kept resisting them. 'My biggest pitfall would be to grab the fat movie contracts, do commercials [and] go on talk shows and be a pompous ass who pretends he knows everything about sex, religion, philosophy, you name it.'

Professionally, though, while offers were also coming in aplenty, they were mostly Benjamin Braddock retreads, all of which he turned down. So, instead of Petrocelli suits and a series of carbon-copy films, he stayed in his two-room West 11th Street apartment with Anne and Karina, dressing in the faded jeans and worn leather motocycle jackets he'd always worn.

Anne, in her own quiet way, had adjustments to make also in accommodating his success into her life. 'The enormity of it scared us both.' she remembered. 'I wasn't ready for people to shove me aside. I was terrified I'd lose him to a starlet.'

During the promotion of *The Graduate*, Anne and Dustin had visited Hollywood, and she made the rounds of studios and talk shows with him, yet even as a first-class sightseer she wasn't impressed. 'I was intimidated by the extravagance. Everyone had their own hairdresser and make-up artist. As a dancer, I was [used to] making $125 a week. We had to wash our own hair and mend our own clothes. I was sure that everyone in Hollywood knew I had holes in my shoes and my underwear. I felt like Plain Jane, and Dustin felt maybe they had made a mistake in choosing him [for the film] in the first place. We were both nervous wrecks and we started fighting with each other . . . I never could get used to seeing his name on a marquee.'

Happily Anne's fear of starlets grabbing her lover were unfounded. Though Dustin may have been attracted to that type of easy affair before his success, afterwards it was another story. Now he needed a woman who was more than just beautiful and sexy: a 'shiksa goddess' was no longer enough. It took Anne a while before she understood that he needed a nurturing, down-to-earth woman and that she had within herself both the sensuality and the basic common sense required. 'Eventually I realized that I didn't have to be "good enough" for him. He picked me.'

Gradually the relationship moved closer to marriage but Dustin was unwilling to make definite plans without some indication of what his professional future would be like. When a reporter visited the pair in July 1968, she asked Anne if she and Dustin would marry. While he was out of the room for a minute, Anne responded by crossing two sets of fingers and holding them high. When Dustin returned, he gave the reporter a few clues as to what he wanted in a wife. 'It's a wonderful thing when you can share a life. I want a wife who can make me laugh, and I would always want her near me.' Obviously a two-career marriage was not something he even vaguely anticipated or wanted. If they were to marry, Anne's career as a dancer would definitely be over. But Anne was in love, so she didn't think about that aspect of her life. She just wanted Dustin happy.

Besides Anne, there was really only one other thing that Dustin needed to feel happy, and that was a good new script. His agents had been shifting through a pile of them but the one that he read and liked the most seemed, at first, the most unlikely. Based on James Leo Herlihy's best-selling novel *Midnight Cowboy*, it was a seamy tale of two lowlife New York City hustlers. Usually an actor who hits it big in one type of picture carefully searches out a follow-up project that will enhance and cement his basic image in the minds of movie-goers, but those actors weren't Dustin Hoffman. As an independent star of the sixties, he was basically a freelancer, able to make any deal or take any part he wanted. In the Hollywood that existed when he was born, virtually every star was under total studio control, and there was no way an actor would have been allowed to depart from an established image – expecially when the image had yet to be solidified: For example, Tyrone Power had been a star at 20th Century Fox for almost a decade before his studio let him make an 'un-image' picture, the gritty drama *Nightmare Alley*, in 1947. And that came only when the studio thought his established screen persona was wearing thin and in need of a change. Unfortunately for Power, he was unable to make a commercially successful change from romantic leading man to character star, but that was not a problem Dustin even thought he had to address. He already was established as a stage character actor and, in his heart, he thought that Benjamin Braddock was a continuation of same. *Midnight Cowboy's* Ratso Rizzo, to him, was just another good part, equally important and challenging as Ben, even though it represented a total turn-around of Ben's image. His friends and agents all advised him to turn it down but Dustin recognized it as virtually an *actor's* dream role and signed to do it for $250,000. The publicity surrounding this career decision only seemed to stablize him as an actor in the eyes of the public, and the money wasn't bad either.

Certainly Dustin needed a quarter of a million dollars just then, but once he got it, it didn't prompt him to spend it all as he'd had to do with his first movie money. In his mind it was an almost incredible sum – almost fifteen times what he was paid for *The Graduate* – but averaged out over his entire acting career, it wasn't really that much money at all. When shooting eventually started on *Midnight Cowboy*, he was still living in the tiny Village apartment that rented for $125 per month. Shortly he and Anne moved to a much larger place directly across West 11th Street which went for some $400 a month, but that was, in part, a gesture of faith as they cautiously moved closer to marriage.

Emotionally, financially and professionally, this was certainly the high-water mark of Dustin's life to date. Before *Cowboy*, he signed to star in a Broadway comedy written by his friend Murray Schisgal entitled *Jimmy Shine*, plus another film at even more money, a romantic comedy called *John and Mary*. It was all the beginning of an intense work period of some eight months.

When asked to comment on all this activity by an interviewer, Dustin said, 'People have me in a little pocket of their minds in that role [of Ben Braddock], and they don't want to see me get out of it. Some people are waiting to see me fall on my ass.'

Whether that was true or just an actor's insecurity, he was taking all logical options to see that it didn't happen. Dustin never settled for being a pocket-sized anything.

# 4

## *The Graduate*
## meets the *Midnight Cowboy*

After years of searching for *one* character in obscure productions from North Dakota to off-Broadway, Dustin, suddenly, had the pick of the lot, juggling, in his mind, three totally different ones at once.

With typical dedication, he chose the most difficult of them, Ratso Rizzo, to dissect mentally and try to understand. Almost immediately he made a minor breakthrough when he developed Ratso's distinctive limp by putting stones in one shoe and then walking on them for a day. His character study continued, without the stones, over some of New York's meanest streets, where he observed Ratso types at every opportunity, mentally adding the crooked limp as an insight into how and why this character came to be the person we first meet onscreen. The limp added a realistically sympathetic touch to an otherwise pathetically unattractive street bum.

In working on the part, Dustin came to realize that he liked Ratso better than he did Benjamin Braddock, finding in him more of the tragedies of life and, therefore, quietly admiring Ratso's struggle to survive in a hostile world. Dustin coupled his own deficiencies with the character's, coming up with insights other actors might have missed. These, coupled with natural curiosity, helped him get a solid grasp on a difficult subject.

'I'd always been fascinated by the people who live on the skid rows of our cities – the ones we regard as the scum of the earth. They're really no different from us . . . only their circumstances. I wanted to get inside one of those people.'

His enthusiasm was echoed by the film's director, John Schlesinger, who admitted that the actor 'made extraordinary sense the first time he read the script [for me]. He also seemed to have the right physical image to play Ratso. Jerry Hellman [the producer] felt the same. Now I can't imagine anyone else playing the part.'

40

Dustin's quick enthusiasm for the picture more than helped the producers to get over the fact that they hadn't got their first choice for the title role, Michael Sarrazin. At the time, Sarrazin was under exclusive contract to Universal Studios, and the amount of money they wanted to loan him out to play Joe Buck, the *'Midnight Cowboy'*, was exorbitantly high so the producers looked elsewhere. Ultimately this would prove to be a major career loss for Sarrazin but a jackpot for another, less known actor.

Among the crop of New York talents considered was Jon Voight, Dustin's old stage pal, who shortly became Joe Buck. Voight had prospered since their old days, most noticeably by winning a Theatre Award for 1967's *That Summer, That Fall.* Like Dustin, Voight had made one grade-Z movie which was yet to be seen, so this was a major career event for him. Joe Buck needed an actor who was rough-looking and not classically handsome, one with a certain naïeté indigenous to the average good-looking New York street hustler. Voight had just that. At thirty-one, he had just the right combination of age, looks and talent to make the part come alive. He would prove to be a perfect counterpoint to Dustin's greasy, streetwise character who does his best to make Joe into a classier act than the just off-the-bus novice we first meet onscreen.

Dustin's character couldn't have been more removed from Ben Braddock, *The Graduate*, but it eventually proved to be just as thought-provoking, concentrating, as it does, on the taboo subjects of homosexuality and male prostitution. Several studios had already passed on the project because of its subject matter, one executive stating it could never be a success because the story 'goes steadily downhill'.

True, the theme of the story did seem a most unlikey topic for a box-office hit, but the acting possibilities were almost endless. It's the tale of a young and none-too-smart Texas boy, Joe Buck, who comes to New York convinced he'll become the city's hottest sex-for-sale stud, only to have his hopes dashed by the impersonality of the people he meets, including, at first, a grasping small-time con artist, Ratso Rizzo. It was not an upbeat story but it was a timely one, since the sixties had opened up various avenues of sexuality, and *Midnight Cowboy* happened to open up a couple of heretofore unrecognized (or unacknow-ledged!) ones.

It proved to be a disturbingly unpleasant experience because the cast were so thoroughly convincing in their parts. Voight/ Buck's descent from self-idealized sex-object to cheap homosexual hustler, aided and abetted by Hoffman/Rizzo as his 'manager', is intensely gripping as the two grow slowly but strongly to depend on each other. Their uneasy rapport on screen was much like that of the audience's to the film itself, drawing viewers into their lives and making them care. Dustin, with his long and greasy hair, filthy white suit and limping gait, seemed a most unlikely screen hero, yet as the film grows in intensity, he grabs the audience and doesn't let go. For Voight, with his squarely bland blond good looks, the sympathy came slower, dampened initially by his strutting cockiness at the opening as he arrives in the big city fully expecting it to fall open at his booted feet.

Audiences really begin to care when Joe and Ratso band together, living in a deserted tenement and, for them both, finally reaching a basic, if temporary, ability to share themselves. Graphically realistic, you could feel the coldness of the New York winter invading their personal slum as Joe opens a can of soup to fortify his ailing friend. When, at last, they leave for Florida, the dream place where Ratzo will wear clean white suits and Joe will seduce every woman in sight, you feel the desperation grabbing at their souls as their bus rumbles down the highway When they finally reach Florida and Joe reaches over to wake Ratso and finds him dead, the despair and waste of both lives hit out with a sledgehamer effect.

Conceived by its producers as basically an art film which would have limited exposure to sophisticated big city audiences, *Cowboy* became instead one of the most popular hits of the summer of 1969. Extraordinary word of mouth promotion brought out sell-out crowds to theatres all over the country.

Just as all this was starting to happen, though, Dustin was somewhat blissfully ignorant, as on 4 May 1969, almost two weeks before the film opened, he and Anne were married and then set out on a European honeymoon. The ceremony took place in Anne's home town of Mount Kisco in Westchester County at Temple Beth Al synagogue and was a small affair.

One can only wonder what was Dustin's parents' reaction to this union between their second son, 'the movie star', and his non-Jewish lover, a divorced ex-ballerina with a small daughter. Dustin, thirty-one was six years older than his bride. Anne's parents were suprisingly liberal about her second marriage. Her father, Frederick, was a librarian at Columbia University, while her mother, Jane, was a schoolteacher, and together they welcomed the Hoffmans into their home for a small reception for thirty-five friends. Though raised as a Catholic, Anne had no qualms about a Jewish marriage, realizing that her commitment to Dustin, nurtured over several years, was more important than any particular ceremony. And with Dustin's career in full swing, the future looked bright indeed.

One of the first stops on their honeymoon was London, where *The Graduate* had yet to become a major hit, so Dustin, for a change, found himself able to walk the city's streets in peace, something he certainly couldn't do at home. There was a part of him, though, which enjoyed the new celebrity, lack of privacy or not, and shortly he was heard singing the popular Simon and Garfunkel song from the film. At one point Anne stopped him and asked if he knew what he was doing.

'No, what?'

'You were singing, "So here's to you, Mrs Robinson . . . hey hey hey, hey hey hey . . .".'

Only a week out of the limelight of his movie success and Dustin missed it. But this was something he never wanted to admit to.

During the on-location filming of *Midnight Cowboy* on the streets of New York, a woman on the sidelines kept waving in front of Dustin a piece of paper she wanted autographed. In character as Ratso and in the middle of a difficult scene, he tried to ignore her, but she wasn't having any of that. 'Mr Hoffman,' she screamed, 'I paid for you,' implying that the price of a ticket to *The Graduate* entitled her to her own little piece of him. He hated the interruption at the time, but in London he found himself missing that kind of attention.

Obviously Dustin's approach/avoidance to his fame stemmed from the days when the short, not good looking 135-pound actor couldn't attract the attention of virtually anyone, let alone sexy women, and he basically distrusted this new attention. They weren't interested in Dustin Hoffman the man but in Dustin Hoffman the movie star. Old wounds heal slowly, if at all. Now, though he was newly married, women were throwing themselves at him, all wanting a slice of *The Graduate*. However, while Dustin admitted he was often tempted, the building of his marriage came first.

After a brief stay in Asia, the newlyweds came home to begin their life together in the Greenwich Village apartment, greeted by the good news of *Cowboy*'s box-office reception. Filmed on the relatively small budget of $2 million and distributed with an X rating, a very rare thing for a major film in 1969, it was already well on its way to making a profit in just the first week of its release.

*Midnight Cowboy* was showing it had remarkable 'legs', building and building its grosses as new audiences discovered it. United Artists president David Picker recalled that, 'When we saw the film one afternoon, we were stunned by its magic and the magic of Hoffman and Voight together. So we decided on a special release pattern – an opening in New York a couple of months before any place else, play-off in small theatres with long engagements, letting word of mouth build an audience.' The project, conceived with bold strokes of initiative and daring, was proving to be a bonanza for all concerned.

Dustin was pleased with his work as Ratso, feeling him a link with the off-beat stage characters of his past. He was comfortable with him, and that showed not only onscreen but in the reviews. For this, only his second major film, the reviewers were again wildly enthusiastic. His searing and sad portrayal of Ratso was deemed 'versatile and gifted, no Mike Nichols creation', by Kauffmann of the *New Republic*. The same reviewers who'd praised *The Graduate* in such glowing terms were raving again.

Hollis Alpert of the *Saturday Review:* 'Hoffman emerges with top honours, proving that his heady debut in *The Graduate* was no fluke.'

*Time* magazine: 'From his debut as the open-faced Benjamin Braddock, Hoffman has progressed by stepping backward – to a supporting part. It is an act of rare skill and rarer generosity.'

Several reviewers, as Mike Nichols had predicted, insisted that Dustin's part was the lesser one of *Midnight Cowboy*, yet he never agreed to that idea. To him, Ratso was the more demanding character, certainly the dramatic equal of Joe Buck, if not more.

The Motion Picture Academy of Arts and Sciences sided with Dustin too, for when the 1969 nominations came out, both Voight and Dustin were nominated for the Best Actor award. The film warranted a slew of other nominations including Best Picture and Best Director (both of which it won), plus one to Sylvia Miles for Best Supporting Actress.

*Midnight Cowboy* made a star of Jon Voight and, to a lesser degree, of Sylvia Miles. As the loudmouthed, wisecracking callgirl, Cass, she literally turned the trick on Joe Buck and from the film emerged as an original screen personality. At thirty-seven, after a long but minor New York stage career, Miles brought her brand of brash believability to her role as the ageing whore in a performance ripe with lewd humour. With her gravelly, cigarette-worn voice and over-the-hill 'Daisy Mae' figure, Sylvia transcended her tiny part to make it one of the most memorable scenes of the film. Lasting only four minutes, her scene in her garish apartment is, unfortunately, usually cut for television showings of the film to exclude her and Joe Buck's frantic love-making punctuated constantly by the images on her television set, the remote controls of which are on the bed beneath her heaving body.

Sylvia's performance has been dubbed a minor classic, and even though she lost the Academy Award to Goldie Hawn's movie debut in *Cactus Flower*, it didn't dampen her spirit for long. She quickly became one of New York's most outrageous party girls, a staple of the gossip columns, and Andy Warhol's newest superstar in *Heat*, his sex-drenched take-off of *Sunset Boulevard*. 'I'm a movie star,' says Syliva, 'and I always get billing over the title.' She has too in several major films including *Farewell My Lovely* (which got her a second Academy nomination). *The Sentinel* and *Evil Under the Sun*, but she has never quite reached the level of 'stardom' many predicted after *Cowboy*. 'Dustin and I didn't have any scenes together but I've known him for a long time because of his stage work. He was wonderful in the picture; he's wonderful in *anything*.' The *noblesse oblige* of one star to another.

Dustin and Voight were also overlooked in the Oscar race in favour of John Wayne's bravura performance in *True Grit*. A touch of irony is that Voight modelled some of his Joe Buck macho image on Wayne. Dustin wasn't as disappointed as he'd been after his first loss. If anything, it was getting to be a habit, but he did start seriously thinking about the basic logic of the Oscars, questioning their validity. After all, how could five totally different performances be pitted against each other with one crowned the best of them? It didn't make sense, and his disenchantment grew steadily over the next few years.

Workwise he accepted a new movie role – and a new image for him – to play a straight, grown-up romantic lead in *John and*

*Mary*. Like his two preceding movies, *John and Mary*, while indeed a romantic comedy, was fastened onto the sixties and that decade's swiftly changing sexual mores. The producers wanted Dustin badly enough to offer him $425,000 and he gladly agreed, especially when he heard the director would be Peter Yates.

Dustin had a soft spot where Yates was concerned because during the Baltimore try-outs of the play *Jimmy Shine*, the director had flown down for initial meetings over their film but then stayed on to help out with the stage production. 'We were in terrible trouble, and Peter came down two or three times and sat up all night with us and made some excellent suggestions. He seemed more interested in helping the play than with planning the movie, and I thought, "This is a real genuine guy".' It was good that Yates did take such an interest in Dustin's play as shortly he would be shooting *John and Mary* during the day while Dustin trod the boards at night in *Jimmy Shine*. Yates understood the possible difficulties of such a situation and made the filming as easy on Dustin as possible.

'Jimmy Shine' was a character cut from the same basic cloth as Benjamin Braddock, a young man in search of a future. Instead of a Beverly Hills mansion, however, Jimmy lived in a warehouse. Exploring his dreams and fantasies in search of personal growth, the character gave Dustin a chance to show off a wealth of comedy abilities including an impression of W. C. Fields.

After a hectic three-week rehearsal period and the brief stint in Baltimore, the play opened in New York on 5 December 1968. Trading on Dustin's hot movie-star status, producer Zev Bufman gladly paid him a weekly salary of $4,500 plus a percentage of the gross *and* half the profits of ever souvenir programme sold. This last detail was worked out between the producer and his star after the programme had been printed. It included some background material that Dustin had not OKd. Instead of having them all reprinted, he settled for half the profits, in the first of many increasingly wise business moves. After years of struggling and money problems, Dustin was already carefully planning for his future.

This time, when *Jimmy Shine* opened, the reviewers didn't haul out superlatives as they'd done for other Hoffman stage performances and the play lasted only 161 performances. While technically not a flop, it was also hardly a hit. *Newsweek*

46

summed it all up when they described it as 'the baddest bad play possible to conceive . . . a mess, an incredibly hackneyed shamelessly exploitive farrago . . .' Happily Dustin barely had time to brood over it as by the time the show closed he was already deep into filming *John and Mary*. In quite a gesture of respect for their star and their investment, the film producers had bought up the matinée performances to give Dustin more breathing space for filming.

It was very generous on Zev Bufman's part to agree to this, but then he's a generous man. When, on the road with the play, Dustin took up shooting pool to relax, Bufman arranged to have a pooltable hoisted up the side of his hotel and installed in the room adjoining Dustin's suite 'You want to please these people,' he explains. 'Limos, aides, redecorating dressing-rooms, flowers and champagne go without saying. It pays off in the end.' Twentieth Century Fox paid off too, paying Bufman some $50,000 for the eight consecutive matinée performances they bought out.

No one intentionally sets out to make a bad movie, and certainly not Dustin Hoffman. On paper, *John and Mary* looked good, especially when Mia Farrow was signed for the female lead. The fey actress was enormously popular at the time, the ultimate Sixties' flowerchild, in fact, but still a novice in the acting department. Certainly her stint on television's *Peyton Place* had helped her learn basic techniques, and the film *Rosemary's Baby* had given her a great chance to be horrified, but she had never played a simple, everyday kind of role. For that matter, neither had Dustin, and after reading the script, he expressed concern about that. 'I have this strong fear that if I am just myself [onscreen], I'm going to be dull.' Expanding on that, he hinted that his penchant for playing cripples and misfits might be crucial to his success, adding, 'The tough thing for me is *not* to have a particular voice or gait for a part.' Would that Mia had stuck to being scared and Dustin to his misfits because as regular young New Yorkers neither was very good. Seeing *John and Mary* today makes you realize that Dustin knew that all along.

Hopelessly bogged down in the argot and mannerisms of the 'Swinging Sixties', the main plot of the film is centred around the idea that, after an entire weekend of casual sex, the two people of the title don't even know each other's last names! Each of their stories is shown mostly in (unhappy) flashbacks

47

between their present situations and how they got there. These glimpses show people so extraordinarily selfish that one can easily realize why they just use first names to newcomers in their lives. Who would *want* to know more?

Shooting on location in New York (with the interiors done at the famed Biograph Studios of silent film days), the producers were looking for an honest look for their film (which they got) and a new screen team capable of the chemistry of the Bogart-Bacall and Hepburn-Tracy pictures of the Forties (which they sadly didn't).

In many scenes Dustin appears frankly nervous, and one can only speculate why. Was he 'acting' his nameless Romeo that way on purpose or was it personal doubts about being able to portray the common Sixties man?

And despite that huge success she'd had in *Rosemary's Baby*, Farrow seemed skittishly anxious, possibly realizing that underneath her fey charm and skinny figure was a lack of bedrock talent?

True there was a certain amount of hesitancy called for in this story of one-night stands but Dustin and Mia seemed immersed in it. Mia, at least, had earned her nervousness even if she overplayed it. The daughter of minor Hollywood royalty (Maureen O'Sullivan and director John Farrow), her romance with Frank Sinatra was enough to make anyone edgy, especially when he dragged two of his old friends, Claudette Colbert and Rosalind Russell, along as chaperones on a pre-marital ocean cruise. The collapse of their marriage in 1968, after less than two years, had added little lustre to either's image or reputation. Sinatra emerged as an ageing Lothario who was no longer able to please a young wife, while Mia came across in the tabloids as a flakey flowerchild whose doe-eyed stare seemed to sum up her personality.

This unlikely twosome was supposed to end up as a top box-office attraction but they were quickly dismissed by audiences who retitled the movie *The Graduate Meets Rosemary's Baby*. Said *Time* magazine about the whole affair, '[It's] as empty as a singles bar on Monday morning.'

# 5

# Stardom and its consequences

Then, just as suddenly as they'd overwhelmed the general consciousness, the Sizzling Sixties were over, leaving a generation of liberated young people high and dry. The 'Me' decade was about to begin, a time that would see the communal values of the sixties swept away into solitary avenues of accomplishment and pursuit, a world far removed from the 'instant emotion' of the preceding ten years. It was a time of change and decision for every one, including Dustin Hoffman. Especially as an icon of the morality of the sixties, thanks to *The Graduate*, *Midnight Cowboy* and, to a lesser degree, *John and Mary*, he had to adapt himself to the changing morality.

True to form, Dustin sought out an exceptional story that had been offered to him several months before, a western, of all things, called *Little Big Man*.

Dustin had read Thomas Berger's best-selling book and was intrigued by the scope and variety of the main character, Jack Crabb, a 121-year-old ancient whose claim to fame is that he's the sole survivor of Custer's Last Stand. The screenplay opens with the wizened man being interviewed about his long life which he proceeds to recall via flashbacks which are a complex but decidedly arousing blend of truth, fiction, fantasy and comedy. It was perhaps the most complicated role Dustin had yet to tackle but he did so willingly in light of the failure of *John and Mary* and his Broadway play. He knew he needed a success, and, though offbeat, the story of Jack Crabb could be it.

As a child survivor of a wagon-train attack, Jack is rescued by the friendly Cheyenne Indians and becomes their adopted son through young adulthood, aided wisely through the years by his 'grandfather', Old Lodge Skins, played with rockhewn authenticity by Chief Dan George. During his first adult battle, he's rediscovered by the white men he's fighting, exposing himself to one during a hand-to-hand fight and being brought back to 'civilization'.

49

The film graphically points up the cultural differences between the placid Indians and the plundering white men coming to take their lands, and in the process, to annihilate as many as possible. The civilization of the Old West that Jack goes back to is a questionable refuge at best. He finds himself taken over by the Reverend Mr Pendrake (Ray Dimas) and his lusciously religious wife, Louise, played by Faye Dunaway. They have a hilarious scene where Dunaway helps out her charge as he takes his first civilized bath, crooning religious slogans as she soaps his wiry young body in obvious appreciation of it. The humour serves to point up the basic hypocrisy of the situation and of the white man in general.

Crabb graduates from Mrs Pendrake's clutches to become, in turn, a protégé of gunfighter Wild Bill Hickock, a patent medicine man offering cures for all ills from the back of his wagon, an alcoholic and dabbler in just about every stratum of society before he finally decides he was happier as an 'Indian' and returns to the tribe that originally sheltered him. After white soldiers massacre his adopted tribe and family, Crabb ends up on the Indians' side at the Battle of Little Big Horn, better known as Custer's Last Stand. (Custer, by the way, was boisterously played by Richard Mulligan.)

The film began with a $5 million budget but by the time the edited 2½ hour film was finished, the total was closer to $10 million, making it one of the most expensive pictures of its time. During the extensive location filming, which ranged from Calgary, Canada, to Nevada and points south, Dustin had his wife and his newly adopted daughter, Karina, by his side. He admitted he didn't enjoy locations alone and missed his family so much that it shortly became standard on every Hoffman picture that the budget included travel and expenses so that his family could come along.

Dustin's Jack Crabb was to prove a most arduous part for him. For his transformation into the 121-year-old, make-up man Dick Smith was called in, and for an average of five hours a day Dustin patiently sat while Smith worked his incredible magic. The make-up was composed of some fourteen latex sections which combined to encase Dustin's head and neck totally. In an effort to save some time in the chair. Smith prepainted the rubber pieces with age spots, veins and capillaries sufficient to convey the character's great age.

All that showed of Dustin's own face were his eyes—and those were disguised with cloudy contact lenses. Despite the complicated and time-consuming process of Dustin's make-up, he really credits it with helping him immensly to pull off the part. 'I felt physically old,' he said, even though the experience itself, extending over several days, was 'the worst I ever went through. I'm not claustrophobic, but I itched and wanted to move every half hour. I wouldn't want to go through it again.' (Words he undoubtedly remembered years later, when he became *Tootsie!*)

Another major problem for the actor was to come up with a voice suitable for his 121-year-old character. Experimenting, he'd lock himself in a room and yell for a couple of hours until his voice was hoarse. That worked but only temporarily. At an old folks' home he tape-recorded one old man but wasn't able to duplicate the sound himself later on. A doctor suggested his taking a drug used in the treatment of alcoholics, but 'I chickened out.'

Ironically one solution came naturally—'I got laryngitis, and I practised with it, played the voice back and it was exactly what I wanted.' However, since he realized he couldn't get sick on cue, he went back to the locked room and started yelling again. 'The next day my voice was OK again. So I screamed while I got dressed, I screamed leaving the room. In the car I rolled up the windows and screamed all the way to the Sawtelle Veterans Hospital,' the location being used to shoot these crucial scenes. The effect, though painful, worked beautifully, and when Crabb recounts his patchworked past, one can barely recognize it's indeed Dustin talking.

Despite its heavy cost and long running-time (which, necessarily, cut down on the number of daily screenings at theaters), *Little Big Man* opened to brisk business. This was a good sign as the rule of thumb is that a film must gross 2½ times its production costs before it can begin to make a profit, and in this case that meant bringing in $25 million to break even. Dustin's performance quickly proved to be a big draw, and a well-received one.

In *Commonweal* magazine, Philip T. Hartung applauded, saying, 'In the title role, Dustin Hoffman gives another of his superb performances', but the *Saturday Review's* Arthur Knight chose to nitpick: 'It is difficult to decide whether Hoffman's portrait of Crabb across generation gaps is a personal triumph for the actor or for the make-up artist who worked cosmetic wonders.' Audiences didn't need to quibble, though, and showed that in the best possible way—by buying tickets.

During his off-hours on distant locations, Dustin and Anne had a chance to indulge in a favourite passtime, collecting antiques. It was a relatively new hobby for him but he enjoyed scouring through dusty shops in search of treasures, and, not incidentally, it was also a good investment. On weekends the couple often ventured up into Connecticut and over to New Jersey, enjoying each other even if they did come up empty. When they did find something, though, it was lovingly added to what was becoming quite an elegant home. Simultaneously he was developing a complementary love for modern paintings, and the Hoffman apartment at 18 West 11th Street was fast becoming a minor museum for his various canvases. Dustin often worked at home so he could enjoy all this, using his large wooden desk set against the wall, in his study, adjoining the townhouse next door.

That Federal-style house had once been owned by lyricist Howard Deitz and was quite a showplace among the graceful brownstones lining the street. Unfortunately the wealthy new owners of the house, Dustin's neighbours, didn't realize the intensity of their teenaged daughter's political leanings: had they done so, a great tragedy might have been avoided. She belonged to an underground group of radicals called the Weathermen, and on a day her family was absent they joined her in the basement of the brownstone to make bombs. They weren't particularly good at it.

Around midday on 5 March 1970 Dustin was at his desk 'going over some negatives of my wedding pictures' when he remembered he'd promised to go to downtown Manhattan with Anne and Karina. They bundled up and left just one half hour before the house next door exploded, blowing itself to pieces along with the group working in the basement. In the debris were found the bodies of two nude young women while the body of a young man was found in the rubble of what remained of the basement. Two more young women were reported as having escaped and gone into hiding. The desk that Dustin had been sitting at scant minutes before the explosion was now dust, just as he would have been had he stayed there a little longer.

The front of his house was blown off and a fire raged through the apartment, quickly eating up most of his collections. When he heard the news, he rushed back to chaos.

By the time he got there, a large crowd had gathered behind the police barricades but Dustin pushed through to see what, if anything, could be saved. He was angry at the crowd, sensing they'd just come to see a show. Here he was, trying to salvage some of his property, while just across the street were dozens of people acting as if they were at a circus.

Until that afternoon Dustin had always felt that his public was basically on his side, supportive of him, but now, in the midst of this personal and private tragedy, he could look out through a shattered window frame and see them laughing and waving up at him. Besides his shock and disappointment, he felt betrayed, commenting with a deserved bitterness that they 'were really knocked out because they were getting their two favourites—a disaster and a celebrity—at the same time.'

Sadly, he was able to salvage only three paintings and a Tiffany lampshade from the mess. Everything else was either destroyed outright or too charred to be restored. He bravely tried to put a good face on it to a friend, quipping 'Thank God, I'm not poor.' Many people were left homeless by the blast and, like the Hoffmans, moved into temporary quarters until they could find a new home. One thing Dustin was certain of, though, was that it wouldn't be in the Village.

Badly shaken, Dustin let Anne look for a new residence while he picked up his career with a script by Herb Gardner. Primarily a Broadway playwright but also a Movie Oscar nominee for his screenplay of *A Thousand Clowns,* Gardner had created the role of a reclusive hit song-writer who lives alone in a penthouse perched on top of the General Motors Building in New York and thinks about death and dying. A bizarre premise, to be sure, but also one that Dustin was attracted to. In fact, he was so interested in it that he helped to bring his old friend Ulu Grosbard into it as director. With Grosbard's help, Dustin hoped to finally be able to carry off a contemporary character, even if he had to be as oddball as Gardner's creation, Georgie Soloway.

George is a talented hack of a song-writer, able to write a military march and an anti-war anthem in the same afternoon. What bothers him most is the fact that his talent is so catholic.. Since it is, how can he really be any good? Georgie is so upset about this that he seeks out a pschyciatrist (Jack Warden) who carefully leads him back through his life from his teenage years to forty, where he faces a decidedly restless mid-life crisis. The flashback sequences gave Dustin a chance to explore Georgie while we all try to understand him.

One of the few highpoints of the film is the too-brief presence of Broadway actress Barbara Harris as a wacky waitress who's been trying for years to make it as a singer. When she meets the famous

Georgie Soloway, she thinks now she'll get her chance to make it big, but their relationship quickly crosses over from professional interest to the personal and we realize that this is the way she's always handled her 'career', thus always dooming it to failure. Their scenes together are the most enjoyable of the film.

The reunion of Dustin and Grosbard was a happy one as they talked about their old days at the Theatre Company of Boston when he'd directed Dustin in *Waiting for Godot*. Grosbard also proved supportive when, in the midst of filming, there was another incident which upset Dustin greatly. It happened when they were shooting late at the General Motors building. 'At about four in the morning, we heard this boom-boom-boom! It was terrorists bombing the Bank of Brazil on Fifth Avenue. I went home and told my wife, "That's twice now they missed me." Dustin had not forgotten the apartment house blast, and the memory of it made him paranoid. Grosbard was able to calm him down, and when the film finished shooting they were better friends than before, even though the end result of all their work, *Who is Harry Kellerman and Why is He Saying Those Terrible Things About Me?*, ended up being hardly worth their effort.

Filming ended in early October of '70, in time for Dustin to help Anne out during the last week of her second pregnancy. When she'd first learned she was expecting a baby, Anne resigned herself to relinquish what dreams remained of her dancing career, choosing instead to get through what was an uncomfortable pregnancy, complicated by having to settle into the family's new home. Furnished with the beginnings of a new antique collection, it was quite a bit larger than the Village apartment. Dustin had taken it with expansion plans in mind, and the first major addition came on 15 October, when his daughter, Jennifer Celia, was born.

Immediately nicknamed Jenna, the baby weighed over eight pounds at birth. Dustin was there, in the hospital with Anne, for the delivery. To him it seemed the ultimate justification of life, not to mention the physical proof of his marriage. At thirty-three, he thought the burbling product of his union marked a new beginning, and he was happy.

After 'the seduction', in *The Graduate*, Mrs Robinson (Anne Bancroft) seems more interested in her nail polish than she does in her bewildered bed partner (Dustin Hoffman)

Ratzo Rizzo (Dustin Hoffman) gives Joe Buck (Jon Voight) the address of his next 'trick' in *Midnight Cowboy*

Director Peter Yates jokes with an animated Mia Farrow and a sleepy Dustin between takes on location in New York City for the ill-fated sex comedy *John and Mary* (1969)

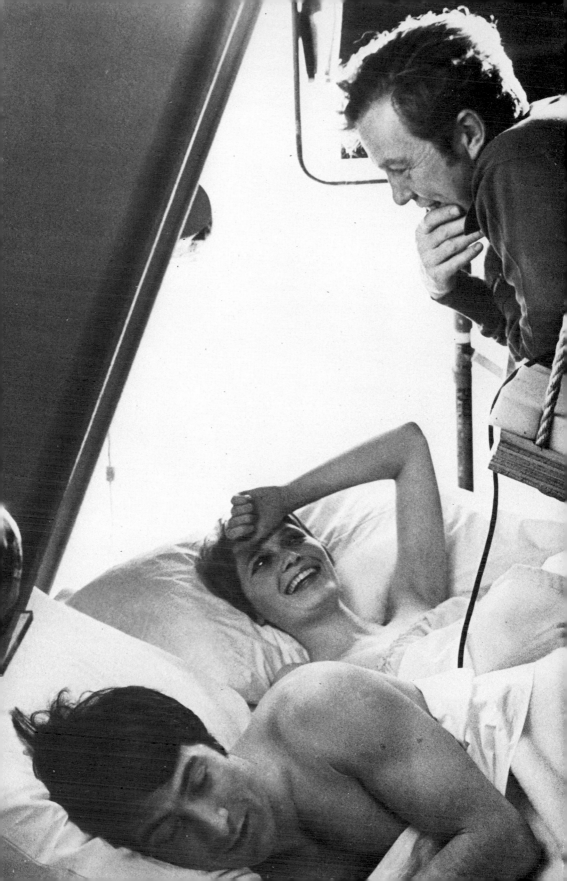

A motherly Mrs Pendrake (Faye Dunaway) shields her new young charge (Dustin) in *Little Big Man*

Raised as an Indian, Jack rides with his beloved 'grandfather', Old Lodge Skins, played by the remarkable Chief Dan George

An ancient Jack Crabb (Dustin) begins recounting the turbulent saga of his life as the *Little Big Man* to a historian (William Hickey)

Georgie Soloway (Dustin) indulges in a wintry fantasy in *Who is Harry Kellerman and Why Is He Saying Those Terrible Things About Me?* Georgie never does find out and audiences couldn't have cared less

David (Dustin Hoffman) faces up to some violent villagers in Sam Peckinpah's overblown morality tale *Straw Dogs* (1972). Due to censorship much has to be cut from the film for television showings but it has proved to be a surprisingly popular offering in the video-cassette marketplace since Peckinpah's death in 1984

Dustin Hoffman as Louis Dega confronts the harsh reality of prison life in *Papillon*

Papillon (Steve McQueen) and Louis Dega get their first glimpse of Devil's Island, in *Papillon*

Dustin and wife Anne share a rare quiet moment together on the set of *Papillon*. Anne was hoping that her small but flashy part in the film would help boost her to stardom

# 6

## Bad moves – *Straw Dogs* and *Alfredo, Alfredo*

Though an established movie name and a respected actor, Dustin had reason to see the up-and-down motions his film career was making. *Little Big Man* had come out to good reviews and box-office after the disastrous flop of *John and Mary*. Now he had to sit back and watch *Big Man's* glow dim perceptibly when *Who is Harry Kellerman . . . ?* was released only to die a quick death at the ticket windows. It seemed that for every right career decision he made, he followed it up with one, that was, at best questionable. As an independent star the choice of what he did was his alone, but his unrelenting search for unusual parts and his increasing sense of perfectionism were making him hard to cast and difficult to work with. Obviously his old lack of self-confidence was still very much with him.

'It's the same old story,' he told a reporter. 'Everyone says that when you reach success, when you've got money and fame, then you've won the battle. The only truth is that life is life, no matter who you are. You're kidding yourself if you say that you're [still] not struggling. It's wonderful being in demand but there are pressures on me now that I never imagined before I became a star. I [still] see an analyst—it's the greatest help in my life.'

It seemed that Dustin's occasional defeats were, in essence, helping him to come to grips with the various devils that plagued him. 'I noticed that I had become obsessed with death after I became famous. I couldn't understand the obsession for a long time and then I realized that, once you're a movie star, you're already dead. You really see life as a vivid dream. It's extraordinary, you have no privacy on the street, which is something you took for granted before.' I saw Dustin and Anne around this time walking up 3rd Avenue in the East 60s in New York, and he looked around at the people, who all recognized him, as if he were a hunted animal and they were all big-game hunters priming their rifles for a shot at him. I remember thinking

55

at the time that it was a shame he wasn't able to enjoy his success and was so ill at ease when he was out among the people who'd made him a star. Certainly they all hadn't been there on 11th Street to watch his house burn and certainly they *all* weren't really that interested in him. And he wasn't stuck with the label of 'star' due to a handsome face but rather it was something he'd once sweated and worked for. He should have been a happy man, but he didn't look like one. Anne, towering over his slouching form, seemed a barricade against anyone foolhardy enough to try to get close.

Or, knowing Dustin's reputation, he could well have been resurrecting Method Acting techniques of paranoia and isolation necessary for a new film. At that time, towards the end of 1970, he decided to accept an offer to work with director Sam Peckinpah, a man whose films specialized in all manner of odd, antisocial behaviour. Peckinpah had reached his greatest fame just two years before, in 1968, with his bloody—but extremely successful—*The Wild Bunch,* a 214-minute western which had starred William Holden, Robert Ryan, Ernest Borgnine, Edmond O'Brien, Ben Johnson and a plethora of other middle-aged movie tough-guys. At that time, reviewers both blessed and cursed the film, calling it everything from a 'controversial landmark' to a 'mindless exercise in violence'. It centered on a group of over-the-hill badmen, *circa* 1913, who are hired by a renegade Mexican general for one last great adventure. Ending in what was called a 'ballet of blood,' some deemed it a surrealistic morality talke while others dismissed it as an excuse for Peckinpah to indulge himself in the kind of physically intense film-making that was his hall-mark.

In any case, its success made Peckinpah a director in demand, and who better to head up his latest production than the star of two other recently controversial films, *The Graduate* and *Midnight Cowboy?* (Cliff Robertson reportedly objected to the violence in the script and turned it down before it ended up at Dustin's door.)

The film, *Straw Dogs,* based on the novel *The Siege of Trencher's Farm,* was being produced by Dan Melnick and partners David Susskind and Leonard Stern of Talent Associates as part of a six-picture deal with ABC-TV's new theatrical movie company.

The idea of a television network producing films which, after theatre release, end up exclusively on their air time sounds good. But the project wasn't thoroughly thought out. Peckinpah's movies have *never* been able to be shown in their entirety on network television because of their violence, the quality which makes them signature Peckinpah movies to begin with. A curious investment for a television network.

And an even more curious end result.

Filmed on location in a desolate corner of Britain, *Straw Dogs* began a ten-week shoot in February 1971. Dustin's co-star was Susan George, a British blonde whose fame rested more on her public love affairs than on her acting ability. A former child actress, her 'mature' roles included such undistinguished items as *Twinky* (1968), *Neat in Black Stockings* ('69), *Die Screaming Marianne* ('70) and *Fright* ('71).

As Amy Sumner, Susan George seemed typecast as the wife of an American mathematics teacher (Hoffman). She brings him back to her home village and proceeds to strut and swagger her bra-less way through town, virtually inciting the locals to riot. When her husband, David, shows up at the local pub, he's ridiculed, then ignored, and events like that continue to pile up to a boiling point where the randy villagers literally attack his farm to get at his wife. David defends his honour, and Amy, in an obvious Peckinpah manner when he blasts away half a dozen of the invaders with a rifle and drives the remainder off after they've broken in and raped her. Peckinpah was such a purist that he actually wanted George to have sexual contact with the movie rapists but she turned him down. He went ahead and got a double to stand in for her.

The point of the picture is that anyone, even a mild-mannered maths professor, would turn to violence if pushed far enough. True or not, seen today, *Straw Dogs'* intense violence and underlying themes of rural alienation seem manufactured and pointlessly unnecessary. Certainly it didn't compel any American intellectuals to take a vacation in Great Britain!

For Dustin, though, it proved strangely therapeutic. The preceding year he'd told an interviewer, 'I'm not a violent person. I don't shoot guns, don't fight, but I get excited by violence. I would like to investigate my feelings about violence in a role.' *Straw Dogs* at least gave him that.

Surprisingly, Dustin also got along extremely well with the demanding Peckinpah, even though 'It was a tough experience [making the film]. But I liked working with him. He had the spontaneity of a child. Suddenly he would come up with things that were very exciting.' He came home feeling good about the project and the esteem that working with Peckinpah would add to his reputation. While Peckinpah went off to Hollywood to edit the film, Dustin was back in New York waiting for good news, convinced he'd be hearing some very soon.

When he'd lost the Academy Award for a second time for *Midnight Cowboy*, Dustin had to console himself with the thought that he would win one when he was ready for it. Early in 1971, after the enthusiastic acceptance of *Little Big Man*, he felt he was. Therefore, when the nominations were announced and he wasn't among the five actors listed, Dustin's growing antipathy towards them became more vocal. He could live without the award, as he'd already proved, but as a businessman, he wanted the prestige of a nomination, knowing full well it would add more clout in future negotiations for his acting services. Although he was situated in the number six slot of the year's Top Ten Box-office attractions, he was still looking ahead. 'I realize that intellectually [the award) doesn't really mean very much. But it is a means to more power, which in turn enables you to be choosy about your scripts. And it makes you more money—which you can put away towards the day when you won't be in such demand.'

Dustin's attitude suggests someone had slipped him a reminder of the *Who is Harry Kellerman . . . ?* reviews—terrible to the last—to help him realize the mistake he'd made in doing it, and that he needed as many good credits, like Oscar nominations, to help producers forget it!

Despite that film and the other stinkers, though, Dustin's hits had indeed made him an international movie star, bringing him to the attention of virtually everyone, including Italian director Pietro Germi.

Germi had made a prestigious *and* funny film some ten years before, in 1961, called *Divorce-Italian Style* which had been a big success in the United States and for which he'd received an Oscar nomination. Two years later his next film, *Seduced and Abandoned*, had been another American hit, but then came a long dry spell. While still one of Italy's top movie-makers, he knew that if he wanted another American hit he had better get an American to star in it. With that in mind, he sent Dustin the script for his latest venture, *Till Divorce Do Us Part*, a satire on Italy's outdated divorce laws.

Long appreciative of Germi's work, Dustin was interested in his offer, especially when Germi threw in the attractive bone of having him serve as co-producer on the film. Thinking this would give him some measure of control over his performance, Dustin's agents agreed for him to star, and the film was set to be made on location in Italy.

Once the agreements were signed, Dustin began a crash course in Italian, studying diligently for several months before leaving for location so he'd be fluent enough to hold his own with his cast members. He had a knack for the language and was anticipating using it in the film so he was deeply disappointed when, upon his arrival, Germi told him that he'd be delivering all his dialogue in English. Germi's reason was that films with English subtitles weren't faring well at American theatres and that audiences there would expect to hear him in his native tongue.

Despite this disappointment for Dustin, filming continued and, again, he actually enjoyed and appreciated his director. 'The pace [of shooting] is very leisurely Germi knows exactly what he wants and cuts as he goes along. He doesn't have to take as many shots and gives more time to each one he wants. Everyone around him is like a member of the family . . . I was the only newcomer to his unit and felt like a new boarder in a rooming-house until I settled in.'

He played a timid bank-teller who meets the girl of his fantasies (Stefania Sandrelli). To his utter disbelief, this vision seems to like him just as much and, in short order, he woos, wins and marries her, only to quickly find out that beneath her gorgeous exterior beats the heart of a shrew. She becomes so domineering that she quickly has him living in the basement while her grotesque parents move in upstairs.

After that sad disillusionment he meets the real woman of his dreams, a down-to-earth architect, and he starts dreaming about a divorce. Faced with the impossibilities of Italian laws, Alfredo's search for a solution to his marital puzzle sets the scene for some low keyed humour and social satire. Dustin was quite pleased with results, even though it was disconcerting to be speaking his dialogue in English while the rest of the cast were speaking Italian.

When the film finally appeared in the United States, though, everyone, including its star, was surprised to hear Dustin's distinctive voice dubbed over by an Italian actor! Critics found this especially disconcerting. One said that Dustin delivered only 'half a performance', while Jay Cocks of *Time* magazine opined that, 'Robbing an actor of his voice is like chopping off an acrobat's legs.'

Eventually the story came out that the film's producers, without Dustin's knowledge, had decided that it would save money simply to dub the film into Italian for international release, and that's just what they did. They added that they would have been delighted to have had Dustin do his own dubbing but, by the time the decision was made, he was long gone back home to other commitments and they couldn't afford to wait for him to be available. In the end, creative decisions had been compromised by the moneymen, a sad but frequent circumstance in film-making.

Yet, while most critics continued carping that Dustin fitted the part about as agreeably as 'a knish in a plate of *pasta fazool*', an important one, Pauline Kael of *The New Yorker*, found it an improvement! 'In general dubbing is an abomination, but the stranger's voice does wonders for Hoffman—it brings him out. In American movies, he's the perennial urban weakling-adolescent, doomed to swallow spit forever, but here, rid of the frightened, choked-up voice that constricts his characters, he gives a softer-edged, more relaxed performance.' Apart from hardcore Hoffmans fans, though, few people found this out as the picture opened and closed swiftly at a few selected 'art' houses in major cities.

More and more Dustin began thinking of ways to have more control over his films, so that episodes like *Alfredo, Alfredo*, the final title of *Till Divorce Do Us Part*, wouldn't happen again. To that end he began considering in earnest an invitation he'd received some time before, to join other top stars who felt the same way—and were doing something about it.

# 7

## The myth of
## career independence

In 1969 three of the most important stars in Hollywood, Paul Newman, Barbra Streisand and Sidney Poitier, joined forces to form First Artists Productions so they would have complete control over their film work. Patterned loosely after the United Artists group of the silent screen era which was formed in 1919 by Mary Pickford, Douglas Fairbanks Sr., director D. W. Griffith and Charlie Chaplin, the new company's main concern was the proper care and feeding (not to mention contracting!) of its stars to their individually best advantage. Each was a superstar despite an occasional flop movie and First Artists was designed to safeguard them from failures. In 1971 Steve McQueen signed up with the group, and Dustin was invited in also.

Since he admired the principals, he was both flattered and intrigued at the prospect of being allied with them. He was also excited at the prospect of having not only built-in safeguards for his movie work but the assurance that he'd have the muscle to demand an optimum fee for a film plus the assurance of a profit participation. The idea was that producers would never resort to creative accounting when they were dealing with a company composed of the most powerful—and profitable—stars in the business. Hoffman's participation was announced in September 1972, and it looked like a most positive step.

Under First Artists terms, he would have total creative control over his films, including the all-important final cut, just as long as that film adhered to these basic rules: it must have a total running time under two hours and ten minutes, be completed according to the budget set before production began, and come in on time, also according to an agreed-upon shooting schedule. Within that simple framework, he enthused, 'You could literally do anything you wanted to do.' To Dustin, contemplating that was like being 'a painter and not just a colour on a palette'.

Immediately he began scouting for properties and building on his new friendship with Steve McQueen. McQueen was getting ready to star in the movie version of the bestseller *Papillon,* which, at that point, was being set up as another in his string of highly popular action-adventure vehicles. When Dustin evinced an interest in the project also, its scriptwriters went to work to create a character for him. By welding together various small ones from the book, they came up with the intriguing Louis Dega, 'the best counterfeiter in France'.

For his efforts Dustin received a salary of $1.2 million, and he and Anne, in high spirits, set off for location shooting in Jamaica, the place standing in for the novel's setting of French Guiana's Devil's Island.

As an added fillip, the writers had also put in a small part for Anne—as Dega's wife! Frankly Anne had missed performing and had long-since found that sitting on the sidelines in the role of the star's wife was not a fulfilling one. She was delighted at the chance to participate in the film, even though her part was really little more than a walk-on. She'd seen the design for the costume in her major scene where she waves here husband off to prison and was delighted to know she'd be looking tall and gorgeous in front of the Technicolor cameras.

The film was budgeted at a whopping $13 million, enough money to make everyone look good, plus director Franklin Schaffner was signed on to direct. Schaffner's coming on board seemed a good omen as he'd recently shepherded George C. Scott to an Academy Award for *Patton.*

Shortly Schaffner would wish for only one thing more, and that was a script as tight and well written as *Patton's,* because that turned into this picture's major problem. Dustin's character proved to be underdone and he became uncomfortable with his part almost from the beginning. Basically the story was McQueen's and the writers knew this, trying to compensate by making Dustin's Louis Dega one with buddy-sympathy, a then popular trend in movies since the success of Paul Newman and Robert Redford in *Butch Cassidy and the Sundance Kid.* Unfortunately it didn't come off in the shooting script, so Dustin, in a period of desperation, began inventing facial tics for Dega, only to have Schaffner spot these improvizations *as* tricks, for they added little to his characterization.

Dustin's frustration with the script, coupled with the physical demands of the picture, caused him to start losing weight, some twenty pounds in all by the time filming was completed. Again, though, one wonders if it wasn't Hoffman the actor at work, subconsciously losing pounds as he worked his way into his character, condemned from a luxurious Parisian life to one of bread and water on Devil's Island. Knowing full well his role was subservient to McQueen's, he could have been trying to make the best of what was left to him.

Adopting a look of utter, slack-jawed terror at the brutality of his fellow prisoners, Dustin/Dega realizes he needs the protection of a stronger man to survive and enlists Papillon's support. Papillon's dreams of escape need subsidizing, and Dega promises him money he's hidden back in France in return for his protection. As a desperate man in an otherwise hopeless situation, he's willing to promise anything to survive. The two stars' on-screen friendship seemed real and honest but there were few Newman-Redford sparks visible in the finished film, an epic which ran some three hours.

Personally, Dustin found himself drawing away from his family, needing progressively more time to leave his character behind and become himself again. 'I have to make a conscious effort to leave those troubles behind.' Yet he embraced those 'troubles' of his shabby, hopeless character and declared that Louis Dega had become one of his most challenging roles. Despite script problems, he ultimately transcended them as an actor, losing himself in the part.

Happily the personal relationship between Dustin and McQueen got increasingly better. Though at first glance a Mutt-and-Jeff friendship seemed likely, the pair ended up admiring each other more and more. In Steve, Dustin saw the rebel and star he'd often wished he could be, whereas in Dustin McQueen saw the actor he'd always longed to be and seldom was in his films, settling instead for superstar status as a sex idol.

To Dustin, Steve McQueen represented the epitome of the 'New York Actor' who'd gone to Hollywood and made it, exactly the opposite of his own career, and he revelled in McQueen's healthy sense of self-confidence. Though McQueen collected cars and motorcycles while Dustin was into antiques and art, they found a concrete meeting ground in their craft and steadily built on that towards a friendship.

As for their $13 million baby, *Papillon*, it too proved a learning experience and a success. When it opened in December 1973, it grossed some $3 million in its first week of release. Despite mixed reviews, the film proved a profitable box-office attraction, and the

McQueen/Hoffman screen partnership proved equally rewarding. Their individual styles of acting blended nicely in the film, with each able to carve out unique characterization, and the reviewers who appreciated their efforts appreciated them a lot. Pauline Kael, only recently a Hoffman suporter was grateful 'each time he turns up, simply because he tried to do something for his characterization.' Taking up from the script's limitations, he'd made Dega almost blind, dependent on his thick glasses for survival in the personal swamp of the penal colony. It was a gimmick that underscored his character's vulnerability, making his alliance with Papillon even more understandable.

McQueen's character of Charrière, 'the butterfly', was much showier and more overtly masculine than Dustin's, which created an off-balance feeling that critics picked up on. After all, Dustin's Dega mostly just stands around while Papillon tries repeatedly to escape the island hell. After eight tries, he finally does escape, and that moment is perhaps the film's most touching. By now they are both old, grizzled and grey, and Dega is finally resigned to his imprisonment, yet agonizing over the fact that he'll be enduring it without his friend. They part on the edge of a cliff as 'the butterfly' make his final leap to freedom.

The whole movie was good old-fashioned adventure but its simplicity was held against it. In *The New Yorker*, Judith Crist said the film 'shows movie-goers that the talents of even Dustin Hoffman and Steve McQueen can be buried under endless restatement of the obvious, and the best adventure stories can be attenuated into boredom'.

To Anne's disappointment, her small part as Dega's wife was mostly overlooked, except to mention that she was Mrs Hoffman, exactly the opposite of what she secretly hoped for.

When all these opinions came out, Dustin reflected on the job he'd done, and then made one of his own: 'I learned not to [try to] build more of a character than the text [of the script] can support.'

Yet millions of tickets were sold, and that was another fact that didn't escape him. His contract stipulated that he'd receive twenty-five per cent of the film's first $500,000 take at the box-office, and then five per cent, of the film's first $14 million gross—and this on top of his $1.2 million salary. By the second month of release the film had already grossed some $15 million, and Dustin was sitting very pretty indeed.

Besides the money, though, as welcome and as well-earned as he considered it, Dustin had a picture in a new genre, the buddy-escapade picture. When it was over, he therefore wanted another change, to take his career in a new direction yet again. He shortly found a project that he hoped would unite fans and critics in unanimous praise—the life, and decidedly hard times, of comedian Lenny Bruce.

# 8

## Perfectionists meet –
## Dustin Hoffman and Bob Fosse

The story of Lenny Bruce was partially one that Dustin Hoffman had lived through. When he first came to New York in the late fifties, Bruce was being hailed as the first of the 'sick comics', a descripton that followed the man from his days in Greenwich Village cabarets until the day he died of a drug overdose. Bruce was a rebel, something Dustin related to, and he was also Jewish and not goodlooking. His saving grace was a remarkable sense of humour, which, though not often appreciated by the masses, kept him alive and thoroughly controversial until his drug problems became public and a wary public backed away. Most importantly, Lenny Bruce was totally unique, with a vocal self-honesty Dustin also well appreciated.

When the film story of Bruce's life first came up, though, Dustin had to struggle with himself before tackling it. He'd seen the Broadway hit, *Lenny*, and was so knocked out by Cliff Gorman's Emmy-winning performance that, initially, he felt no one else could play the part. Which is exactly what he told the film's producers when they first approached him. He also felt the script they asked him to read exploited Bruce's sad life instead of making it emotionally understandable, and so he sent it back.

Rumours then began that Dustin would make his initial film for First Artists based on the novel *Friday, the Rabbi Slept Late*, a comic outing that would have him playing a rabbi-turned-detective—an intriguing premise—but the negotiations quickly fell apart, bringing Dustin back to the project he really was interested in.

In the meantime the producers had signed Bob Fosse as director of the project, and he wanted Dustin so badly for it that he started rewriting the script himself while launching a personal campaign to bring Dustin aboard. In public Fosse would fall to his knees with his arms outstretched Jolsen-style, pleading with him to reconsider. And he wasn't joking.

Dustin read the new version of the script but didn't make a commitment until it was announced that Al Pacino was close to signing a contract. Then Dustin said yes. (Gorman had also been in the running but the producers felt, as they so often do, that, despite his Broadway success, he wasn't a big enough 'name' to carry off the film.) Pacino was then enjoying the kind of overnight success that Dustin had experienced after *The Graduate*, and, to make matters worse, his talent and looks were constantly being compared to Dustin's, a fact he wasn't all that happy about. (In retrospect, one wonders if Fosse didn't have a hand in these particular rumours, being the expert that he was at getting what he wanted by whatever means necessary.)

The new script written by Fosse (with no screen credit) helped Dustin feel assured that the movie would do Bruce's life the justice and compassion it deserved. Not only did he feel a deep kinship with the late comic, but he also felt one with Fosse as he recognized in him a shared dedication in getting what he wanted up there on the screen.

Fosse was a director who'd proved to be both sensitive and commercial. In 1973 he won an unprecedented Triple Crown, a Best Director Oscar for *Cabaret*, a Tony Award for the Broadway musical *Pippin*, and a television Emmy for Liza Minelli's spiritedly breathtaking special *Liza With A Z*—and he was an unabashed workaholic to boot, whose career had spanned a period as an MGM movie chorusboy in the early fifties to staging such Broadway hits as *The Pajama Game* and *Sweet Charity*. Each of those shows he turned in to highly regarded and popular films, and he was ready for the challenge of *Lenny*.

A chainsmoker who'd often go through five packs a day, Fosse worried constantly about how this movie would fare. Was it too downbeat? Would Bruce's four-letter language be too offensive? Was the project too elitist to find a commercial audience? Could he pull it off? About the only thing he was sure of was Dustin, as he worked night and day getting the films ready to go.

While this was going on, Dustin was doing his homework. Once he'd decided to play Lenny Bruce, he began immersing himself in the man's life, buying and listening to the records the comic had made, watching old television shows he'd appeared on (what few there were), reading all available newspaper material and talking to his old friends. As he learned facts about the man, Dustin dutifully logged them on three-by-five-inch index cards so he could constantly pull them out to study.

And Bruce's life and career were indeed something to study. His 'sick comic' reputation was earned by his penchant for using 'obscene' language while describing comic situations centred around the issues of the day. No subject was off limits to poke fun at, 'niggers' and masturbation being only two of his favourite targets. His onstage mission, as he saw it, was that everyone was already thinking about these subjects so why not be up front and make people laugh about them, as Bruce knew that laughter was the first step to acceptance and understanding. Unfortunately, as one of the first people to do this, he suffered the social consequences. He made enemies among the establishment and even among the intellectuals who'd initially flocked to him. Later, when he became addicted to drugs (certainly another fifties 'unmentionable') and was arrested, there were few who tried to save him. His mission turned into a reservoir of personal pain and disenchantment with both society and one individual's ability to change it.

In his own way Dustin empathized with Bruce the more he got to know of him, with Fosse right there to help. And if Fosse proved to be the strict perfectionist that he was rumoured to be, Dustin was ready to accept that to make everything work.

Fosse's reputation as a starmaker had been established with his Broadway hits and, in movies, with Liza Minelli in *Cabaret*, so to actresses at large the role of Lenny's wife, Honey Bruce, was a most desirable one. The part called for a combination of earthy sexuality and inner sensitivity, qualities that look simple on paper but are hard to find in reality, as Fosse quickly found out.

For a time it looked as if Joey Heatherton was Fosse's choice for the part. The pert blonde starlet had done some decent acting in a minor film or two but was also a trained stage dancer as well. Yet, as rumours peaked, Fosse did a turn-around and cast leggy Valerie Perrine as Honey. Perrine had won rave reviews in 1972's film version of Kurt Vonnegutt Jr.'s bestselling novel *Slaughterhouse Five*, though, admittedly, many of those reviews had centred on her spectacular looks rather than acting talent. *Slaughterhouse Five* was a critically successful movie that failed to find a large audience, and it's to Fosse's credit that he even saw it, let alone recognized that beneath Perrine's glorious exterior lurked a real, if specialized, talent. Yet, as he shortly found out, that was Fosse's great gift.

One pivotal scene comes when Honey is being sentenced to prison on a drug charge, and to make sure she projected just the right sense of horror and despair, Fosse came up to her just before calling 'action' and told her that her boyfriend had just died in an aeroplane crash! Close to hysteria, Perrine nonetheless went on with the scene and did a remarkable job. (Perhaps Fosse remembered another director who, to get the same kind of emotional effect, sneaked up on the child star Margaret O'Brien during *Meet Me in St Louis* and whispered that her dog had been run over by a car, ending with a scene containing that same kind of heartbreaking realism.)

During the sixteen weeks the cast and crew spent in Florida in early '74, Fosse wasn't any easier on his star either. To get the effect he wanted, he risked Dustin's anger on many occasions, but Dustin's commitment to the movie helped him draw on reserves of patience he probably didn't know he had. 'He had me doing this routine where Lenny is talking lickety-split. Take after take, he said, 'Faster. Faster.' I said nobody talks like this. I got very angry at him. It was like twenty takes. He'd break you down after a series of takes so you didn't know which end was up, and he'd always get what he wanted. And he was absolutely right. He wants you to do your best. He's an obsessed leprechaun; I think he is always sitting on your shoulder, whispering in your ear.'

The major challenge to both actor and director came when it was time for Dustin to recreate Lenny Bruce on stage. And even though they were meant to be comedy routines, Dustin found them no laughing matter. True he'd been studying Lenny almost microscopically, finding his mother, Sally Marr, the best person to help him gain insight to the real person. On stage, though, was a different matter entirely, and as malleable and adventurous an actor as he was, Dustin was scared. He'd never seen Bruce on stage himself because in those days he was too busy saving money for the rent to have any to spend in Village nightclubs.

Fosse decided that he wanted Dustin's standup comedy scenes to be as real as possible and make arrangements to film several of them in actual Miami nightspots, using an invited list of people as the live audience. The idea of doing the classic Bruce monologues in front of people, even if they were carefully selected strangers, left Dustin's mouth dry, and it took a persistent Fosse to get him out there. At one point his insistence caused Dustin to blow up, yet Fosse was neither discouraged nor angry at his four-letter word outbursts. 'Dustin had never done anything like this before. The audience was making him nervous, so I put the cameras on him, and we rapped back and forth like a television warm-up. It is much easier for performers to become actors. It is more difficult to make an actor become a performer.'

Fosse did not limit his criticisms to his star, however, as even extras in the film found out. Not satisfied with the reaction of one member of the audience to Dustin's routines, he chastized the guy in front of the entire company, then yelled 'Action', and the shocked face of the man can still be seen in the film today.

The location shooting in Florida coincided with some of its hottest weather, a factor that strained tempers to the breaking point, making it an uncomfortable experience for everybody. Fosse liked working with the raw nerves of his actors though and tried making the situation work for him. During one love scene filmed in a hotel bedroom, Dustin swore the temperature was well over a hundred degrees and lamented that they weren't filming in a modern studio. 'They had to seal up the room, and air-conditioning couldn't be used because it would hurt the sound. Here we were baking and sweating and doing this love scene together and we couldn't even see straight.' That was exactly why Fosse had picked that location, and what ended up on film was just the realism he was looking for.

Fosse's eccentricities ultimately proved worthwhile when the film was assembled and seen for the first time. As a whole it was remarkable, and Dustin was extraordinary. His first close-up shows a very young and innocent face which we see become more ravaged and disillusioned as Bruce's life unfolds on screen. The drug scenes, in the stylistic black-and-white photography, are every bit as graphic as had ever been seen before, easily rivalling *Lady Sings the Blues* in their intensity.

Dustin's performance easily captured Bruce's spirit and mannerisms, showing him as both cult hero and social villian in a balancing-act of great subtlety. Through Dustin, the audience begins to understand what comedy meant to Lenny Bruce and what he meant to comedy. As we see him impersonate Lenny and repeat his classic routines, one realizes that without Bruce's daring originality the face of comedy would be very different today.

Much later Dustin would say that he wasn't happy with what he'd done in *Lenny*, calling it 'a flawed work', but upon its release he won critical raves for it. Though split on the merits of the film itself, critics rallied round Dustin. *Time* magazine's Richard Schickel thought the film didn't face up to the realities of its subject but that Hoffman was 'again asserting his claim to being today's great character leading man . . . he gives a complex and mercurial performance.' *The Hollywood Reporter* went a step further, stating that the movie 'could well boast that Dustin Hoffman *is* Lenny, for his performance is unique and compelling'.

Dustin's quest for a project that would unite critics and audiences in his favour didn't quite work out this time, but the film went on to be one of the most applauded of the year, garnering a total of six Academy Award nominations, including the top four of Best Picture, Best Actor, Dustin's third nomination, Best Actress for Perrine, and Best Director for Fosse. At the award ceremony on 8 April, 1975, however, the film came a cropper, winning none of them. Naturally Dustin was disappointed, but this time it was for Bob Fosse in light of what he'd just been through.

Fosse's driving perfectionism had ultimately proved to be much harder on himself than it ever had been on his stars. Besides his chainsmoking, he freely confessed to other addictions as well. 'I did cocaine and a lot of Dexedrine. I'd wake up in the morning, pop a pill. After lunch, when I couldn't get going, I'd pop another one, and if I wanted to work all night, still another one. There was a certain romanticism about that stuff. There was Bob drinking and smoking and turning out good work. Still popping [pills] and screwing around with the girls. "Isn't it terrific macho be-haviour," they'd say. I probably thought I was indestructible.'

He wasn't and during the editing of *Lenny* and the preparation of a new Broadway show, *Chicago*, Fosse suffered a major heart attack that was almost fatal. His recovery was long and slow and involved a total change of lifestyle and readjustment. (True to form, though, he later used all his personal torment and fears of death in another film, *All That Jazz*.) At the time of the awards he was still convalescing, and Dustin put aside his own desire to win to root for his director, making the outcome even more disappointing.

The loss of the Awards, though, was offset by the fact that *Lenny* was proving to be a box-office success. This, plus Fosse's illness, helped to temper Dustin's remembrances of the rough location shooting in Florida. Fosse's own sacrifices in getting the film right seemed so much more valid than the memory of an occasionally sweaty set! He kept in close touch by phone on Fosse's recuperation, saying, 'He's a very fair man . . . a very hard-working director, and there are some things he doesn't tolerate. He drives himself to death literally and he doesn't tolerate it when a person doesn't do his job. He's not only someone who's gifted

71

but someone who works hard.' Those were qualities he recognized in himself and therefore understood and appreciated in others. Even if it often took him time to realize it!

Also Dustin was intrigued by Fosse's close brush with death—death still being one of his favourite subjects. Seeing his near escape while in pursuit of professional perfection helped fuel Dustin's resolve in realizing another dream of his own, that of directing a Broadway play. Even before the critical and financial results of *Lenny* were in, Dustin made a personal commitment to this and turned to his old friend Murray Schisgal for advice.

Once that decision was made in his head, Dustin acted on it. He realized it would mean giving up films for a while but he remained adamant, turning down *Five Easy Pieces* (possibly a mistake considering what it did for Jack Nicholson) and an offer from Italian director Franco Zefferelli to play Christ in a proposed television epic. His slate was cleared for a journey in a new direction.

# 9

## Broadway again –
## this time in the director's chair

While Dustin had certainly proved himself to be a bankable movie star, his record of success on Broadway, after the flop of *Jimmy Shine*, was another matter entirely. When he decided to go ahead as the director of a Broadway show, the news was greeted with mixed reactions. Many of the more dedicated thought that he'd deserted the sometimes barren landscape of the theatre for the moneyed hills of Hollywood and resented that he felt he could simply drop back in whenever the spirit moved him.

Before casting could even begin, production money had to be found for the project, a comedy revue entitled *All Over Town*, written by Dustin's pal Murray Schisgal. That proved to be no easy feat. When first written it was submitted to over half a dozen seasoned Broadway producers, and some seven of them were interested in mounting it, but one by one they dropped out, leaving Dustin distinctly disillusioned at the vagaries of the business side of the theatre. Yet, adhering to his own basic rule of challenge/survival/success, he plunged ahead, going as far afield as Washington's Kennedy Center for backing, but they also turned him down.

His old mentor, Joseph E. Levine, who'd made millions on *The Graduate*, came to Dustin's aid by offering to put up $100,000, and shortly Adela Holzer, the producer of *Hair*, also joined the group. It soon proved to be an uneasy alliance, however, with Levine and Dustin arguing over details of the show, and Levine subsequently dropping out entirely. Dustin had likened finding the production money to a crapshoot, and was frankly getting tired of the game. However, his faith in the project prompted him to call on his old friend Gene Hackman, whose star, like Dustin's, had risen to lofty heights. Together they raided their respective bank accounts to find the estimated $300,000 necessary to launch the show.

Once the money aspect of the project was finalized, Dustin found there were other problems to be dealt with.

While Broadway grumbled and gossiped about his financial dealings, the tabloids began hinting he was having personal difficulties as well. It was no secret that Anne was underwhelmed by her screen debut in *Papillon*, taking it personally when reviewers overlooked her entirely, unless adding a footnote pointing out she was Mrs Hoffman. True, her part in the film was a very small one but her striking visual impression seemed certainly strong enough to attract other producers to explore her talents at least. When no such interest was forthcoming, she felt ignored and angry. Also it was no secret that her desire to get back into showbusiness was not resting well with her husband, especially after the birth of their daughter. Anne was feeling more and more hemmed in by her marriage and by being nothing more than 'The Star's Wife'. She'd been that long enough to know it didn't count for much, and her long years and dedication to her dancing technique now seemed useful for little else but making graceful entrances at movie premières and parties.

And Dustin wasn't helping the situation. Getting her the small part in *Papillon* had been an indulgence for him and was supposed to be a lark for Anne. Little did he know at the time that it would rekindle her ambition for a professional identity of her own. Adding fuel to this smouldering fire were wild rumours that he had indeed left Anne and moved into an Oakland, California, commune with a young female art student. Those rumours were quickly dispelled but they started heads nodding just the same. And to top off all this talk of marital unrest was the resurgence of Dustin's long-dormant streak of womanizing.

One of the many actresses to audition for *'All Over Town'* was a young woman named Meryl Streep, who found out about Dustin's habits very early on. In an interview, the lady who would eventually play Dustin's estranged wife in *Kramer vs. Kramer* said, 'He came up to me and said, "I'm Dustin-burp-Hoffman," and he put his hand on my breast. "What an obnoxious pig," I thought.' For whatever reason, Meryl didn't end up in the cast of *All Over Town*.

Recalling his own long struggle to get his acting career launched, Dustin was extremely generous in auditioning newcomers. In fact, he saw just about anybody who showed up, including untried beginners and a few taxicab drivers! Anybody who might possibly have something to contribute was welcome, and in all he saw almost fifteen hundred actors.

Eventually, after the sorting of eight-by-ten glossies and the sifting of hundreds of resumés, Dustin chose Cleavon Little for the lead. The young black star had won a Tony award in 1970 for his bravura performance in the musical *Purlie* and was deemed just right to play a crafty opportunist in this new comedy about big city life. The excellent Barnard Hughes was signed to play a senile psychiatrist, Zane Lasky as a sex-happy ladies' man, and Pamela Payton-Wright as the *ingenue* who grows up in a hurry.

With all the characters in *All Over Town*, Dustin at last had a blanket opportunity to start using the nuggets of directional knowledge he had gleaned over the years from such masters as Lee Strasberg, Mike Nichols, Ulu Grosbard and Bob Fosse. (Before they had worked together in *Lenny* he once spent three nights running watching Fosse rehearse *Pippin*.)

As a sensitive actor who'd undergone the heat of being directed by these variously strict taskmasters, he set out to be as understanding as possible of his large cast, going out of his way to offer encouragement whenever it was possible. Also, as directors had allowed *him*. He was willing to listen to his actors, hoping, and occasionally finding a small insight here or there that served to flesh out and make a character more believable. He didn't hand out praise easily—he'd received too many kicks in the rear end for that—but when he felt it was earned, he was lavish with it. His actors appreciated that fact and knew when they did hear a good word, they'd earned it! When hints of Dustin's critical largesse began to become known, he quickly dismissed any so-called generosity, saying directing actors was like guiding children. After all, one good rumour could well have undone his reputation as a hard-driving perfectionist.

During the four weeks of rehearsal Dustin tried to shepherd his sixteen actors into a precise company, yet, when they opened in Chicago during the third week in August of 1975, the results were far from encouraging. Immediately he and Schisgal put their heads together to help solve some obvious script problems—problems that materialized only under the scrutiny of a paying audience. Dustin quickly proved, though, that he was a director who could not only give his company direction but take it as well. The disappointing Chicago reviews were virtual blue-prints to him, and he laboured many hours shifting and shuttling characters in re-sculpting the show.

When they finally brought it into New York, those changes seemed to have paid off. *Time* magazine, a publication usually in Dustin's corner, proved so again when, in reviewing the play, it commented that his time spent with Mike Nichols on *The Graduate* had indeed been well spent and that some of Nichols' unique comedic ability seemed to have rubbed off. Most of the reviewers spent more time commenting on the show's director than on story and substance, and when they *did* concentrate on the story, they found it funny but cluttered by too many actors in search of the next punchline.

*All Over Town* didn't last long on Broadway, but by then Dustin was looking at the project in a more equable light. Instead of the play being a life-or-death landmark, he tempered his views, seeing the whole thing as a learning experience from which he was determined to walk away a better man. Not that he was willing to admit it had been a picnic. 'I did find things I didn't like about the experience: having to work with so many actors, for one thing. Next time I would prefer a half-dozen actors who were really together. The way Broadway is set up, an actor can't think of it as just a job. Everyone had to work more hours than in a day to make it.'

So, at first glance, 1975 didn't look like Dustin's year. He'd found that Broadway wasn't his for the asking, and when he lost the Oscar for Lenny to Art Carney's *Harry and Tonto,* he certainly felt little better about the machinations of Hollywood. The good news, though, was that he was listed among the top five male stars at the box office, right up there along with John Wayne, Burt Reynolds, Robert Redford and Paul Newman. That, to Dustin, was something to be proud of. The Academy Awards committee and Broadway critics and moneymen be damned, because Dustin realized where his appeal lay and quickly found a new project to prove it again.

# 10

# All the President's Men

Robert Redford was the man who first saw the film possibilities of *All the President's Men*, the best selling Watergate exposé written by *Washington Post* reporters Bob Woodward and Carl Bernstein. After his critically acclaimed role as *The Candidate* in that hard-hitting drama of political engineering, Redford had become extremely interested in the Watergate bugging scandal which had started surfacing in 1972 and then spilled over the front pages and airwaves of the world for many months to come. His determined public interest stance, which has increased over the years, was then just beginning to be an important motivating force in his life, and when he heard about the two young reporters work in unmasking the Republican cover-up of the Democratic election headquarters break-in at Washington's Watergate Hotel, he was immediately intrigued, feeling it could make a timely and thought-provoking film.

Acting on instinct, Redford contacted Woodward and Bernstein and committed himself to a film, optioning their book for his production company long before it became an international success. Dustin came to the project later, after he'd read the book, and saw in the character of Carl Bernstein a chance to finally play an all-American hero. After the tortured Lenny Bruce, he needed a complete character reversal—a 'good' Jew after Lenny's 'bad' one. And in Bernstein he figured he'd found a nice Jewish boy who, (almost) singlehandedly, unmasks the political scandal of the century.

Once the book was out, Dustin approached the authors with an offer of some $400,000 to option their property, only to find that Redford's Wildwood Enterprises production company had beaten him to it. Luckily, Redford envisioned the movie much as Dustin had and he couldn't think of a better actor to play Bernstein than Dustin. Accordingly, he offered him the part. Said Dustin, ' I thought you'd never ask.'

By then there was a script almost ready, written by William Goldman, who'd scored greatly with 1969's *Butch Cassidy and the Sundance Kid* which had starred Redford and Paul Newman. Since then Goldman had also worked with Redford on *The Hot Rock* in 1972 and, three years later, *The Great Waldo Pepper*.

Goldman had looked forward with relish to writing the screenplay for *President's Men* and after a long period of work was finally happy with the results. Therefore he was greatly surprised when Bernstein showed up one day, shortly before filming began, with a screenplay of his own, written with his then wife the writer Nora Ephron. Rumours started clouding the acceptability of Goldman's script, that it wasn't good enough, and it took several tense weeks to smooth everyone's ruffled feathers. The result was that the much-discussed 'second script' cast an uneasy light on Goldman's, and the film went into production under a haze of uncertainty and under the direction of Alan Pakula. The combination of script 'troubles', the two intense superstars heading up the movie, and the potential social impact of the story itself, made it, according to Goldman, 'the biggest gossip picture since *The Godfather*'.

Right from the beginning, *All The President's Men* was a picture that people wanted to see. Not only did it showcase two superstars, but it would also, and perhaps *finally*, make some sense of the Watergate mess for the millions of people who'd otherwise tried to avoid it. And with Redford and Hoffman, they'd not only be getting a national crisis but glamour to boot, with Redford perfectly cast as the WASP-ish Bob Woodward and Dustin ideally suited as scrappy Carl Bernstein. Like *Tootsie* years later, it was the kind of picture whose every production move and temperament was duly noted in popular newspapers and movie-trade publications, giving it the kind of publicity overdose that could either help it as a hit or make it a memorable joke.

The mid-seventies were littered with 'front-page' productions, and it had often proved to be a mixed blessing at best. Redford's own *The Great Gatsby* was arguably the most publicized and oversold picture of its year (1974), with its producers capitalizing on the Gatsby legend with a line of merchandising tie-ins which included everything from bed linen to vodka. Unfortunately the film itself received miserable reviews and equally sad box-office receipts, despite Redford's much-heralded sex appeal.

Then Dino de Laurentiis got into the act with his *King Kong* remake which starred then-model Jessica Lange. It too, despite an incredible publicity barrage, was virtually murdered by reviewers and then buried by what few audiences there were who actually saw it. Jessica Lange forgot all about a movie career for several years, while all concerned tried to forget *King Kong*. One of the few exceptions of *Superman* in 1977, but that was a rare peacock in a field of cinematic turkeys.

At the offset, the producers of *All The President's Men*, Redford and Walter Coblenz, were determined that their film would side-step any kind of circus atmosphere the Press might engender and, with that determination to maintain a top level of dramatic integrity, they hired Alan J. Pakula as director. Pakula, then forty eight, had first risen to prominence as the producer of such intelligently received films as *To Kill a Mockingbird* and *Love With the Proper Stranger*, in 1963, going on to enhance his reputation with a series of thoughtful dramas including the cult-classic *Inside Daisy Clover* (1966), which contains Natalie Wood's finest performance, *Up the Down Staircase* (1967) and, as producer-director, *The Sterile Cuckoo*, in '69, the film that made Liza Minelli a movie star. His *Klute*, in 1971, brought Jane Fonda to an Oscar for her portrayal of a callgirl stalked by a killer, and in '74 he'd touched base with American politics with *The Parallax View*, an intense and well-received thriller starring Warren Beatty. (Another advantage was that since Pakula had worked so well with these 'temperaments' as stars of his films, he would also be able to juggle egos of all sizes on *President's Men*.)

Thus insured, the producers were confident that despite what the media might report they'd be putting together an honest and worthwhile film. Redford was delighted when he learned that Dustin had long admired Pakula and was eager to work with him, a very good omen since it immediately defused any rumours of possible star-director conflict.

All agreed from the start that authenticity was the key to telling the Watergate story. For starters, Dustin began hanging out with and observing a newspaper reporter in Maryland to get the feeling of the daily routine of reporting, while Warner Bros combined two soundstages, some 33,000 square feet in all, to recreate the *Washington Post's* city room—at a cost close to $500,000. So accurate were they that several tons of real *Post* trash, everything from bent paperclips to empty cigarette packs, was brought to the Warners' lot to 'decorate' the set.

Hoffman walked away from his brief internship a wiser man. 'I couldn't get over the fact that the paper really does get out every day. Except for a few flurries of activity, it's as quiet as an insurance company. But it's also the *pleasantest* environment I've ever spent any time in.' A nice experience, perhaps, but one not of particular use, since the script had been purposely designed for Dustin to carry much of the investigative brunt of Carl Bernstein's detective work. After letting his hair grow to a shaggy length, he bore an uncanny resemblance to Bernstein, which was another plus for the film. Happily Dustin and his off-screen counterpart got along well, because Dustin often sought out Bernstein's advice to settle points of discussion as to how things got done in the newspaper business.

Redford, too, was often on the phone to Bob Woodward, making sure that just the right attitude and emotions were coming across in the give-and-take relationship of the star/reporters. Goldman's script, as it had been in real life, tossed more of the gritty, hard-nosed scenes in Dustin's direction, letting Redford's gather most of the necessary audience sympathy. Afterall, Woodward and Bernstein were partly responsible for the downfall of a president, and it was necessary to build up a certain amount of audience identification to counter publicity that called them glory-seeking reporters whose success was based on a wild chance of luck.

As with Bernstein, Woodward's character was buttressed by personal details to help solidify his image in Redford's mind. In fact, the prop telephone Redford used on the set desk had Woodward's real 1972 phone number on it!

Realizing the picture would be a magnet for publicity anyway, Dustin and Redford made a rare move when they showed up on the set the day that the *Post's* 'newsroom' was unveiled at Warner Brothers, happily greeting dozens of reporters and even conducting a few guided tours around the mammoth double soundstage. They figured that since there'd be publicity anyway they might as well do their part to make it as accurate as possible and a plus for the picture.

Ironically, one of the places where they *didn't* expect to receive much support was from the head office of the *Washington Post* itself. Editor-in-chief Katherine Graham had expressed doubts about the project from the beginning. She felt that 'Hollywood' was invading her private preserve of serious journalism and frankly resented the intense hullabaloo unleashed by the Woodward/Bernstein book in general. Her personal downgrading of the movie eventually hampered the film-makers as they found more and more *Post* employees unwilling to talk about the

Watergate affair. Graham's position was strengthened when she learned that Goldman's script had been written as an openly commercial entertainment—as it should have been—and was initially pleased when she learned that Carl Bernstein was writing a script of his own.

Goldman, however, was aghast at Bernstein's script attempt, finding it little more than a personal accounting of his romantic adventures, (ironically, Bernstein had written it with his then girl-friend, Nora Ehpron, who went on to become his wife, albeit briefly.) After several conferences to calm everyone down, Goldman's script was given approval, and that's what went before the cameras. Dustin was very enthusiastic about this script and its outlook. 'The movie doesn't have so much to do with what Watergate was, as with what it represents symbolically. I (personally) just resist the symbol of the picture of Watergate because [the film] is more about the newspaper business and how it functions and how it operates.' Instead of being a plodding story of behind-the-scenes political manoeuvring, the film was constructed to show aspects of that coupled with being a wide-eyed whodunit as the principals become as aghast as the audience as they painstakingly uncover the sleazy underbelly of Watergate.

True to the tradition of his *Butch Cassidy and the Sundance Kid* screenplay, Goldman injected a fair amount of wry humour into the proceedings which served to establish the initially rocky partnership of Woodward and Bernstein and, later, to reinforce their growing commitment to the story. When stories of the humorous aspect surfaced, they further disenchanted *Post* publisher Kay Graham and her employees.

Redford and company didn't let that negativism get to them, and the shooting of the film was completed in only ninety-six days, an exceptionally short time considering the numerous Washington DC locations. If anything, the apathy they encountered there only spurred them on to do better work, although at one point Dustin became so incensed at the lack of *Post* co-operation that he went to Redford and Pakula to ask them to rename the paper in the film. They managed to calm him down, and shooting swiftly continued. If anything, this mini-controversy only served to add more clippings to the film's burgeoning Press files.

Despite the fact that the script had worked out to everyone's satisfaction, rumours of 'problems' continued in the classic manner of Hollywood gossip: if you can't find something new to say, rewrite and say it again. Happily, unlike *King Kong* and *The Great Gatsby*, *All the President's Men* was able to maintain its image as a serious film work and not fall into the 'joke-of-the-week' movie category attached to *Kong* and *Gatsby* long before they had even been released. True the public heard plenty about *President's Men*, but the talk only served to whet the appetite of the ticket-buyers.

To ensure that everyone would be able to satisfy their curiosity about the film as quickly as possible, Warner Brothers opened the film on 8 April 1976 in over five hundred theatres across the country. In recent years this 'wall-to-wall' opening pattern has evolved from its humble beginnings when Joseph E. Levine instituted it to sell his 1957 Italian-made *Hercules*, spending more money on prints of the movie than was used to produce it! Levine's logic was to get the film into as many theatres as possible, as *fast* as possible, before word-of-mouth spread as to just how bad a film it was. It worked for Levine, helping him found the mini-movie empire that eventually gave him the money and clout to make *The Graduate*.

Since then, producers have used this system of blanket release with varying results. Unfortunately for their producers, both *King Kong* and *The Great Gatsby* fell into the *Hercules* grab-the-money-and-run category, while such films as *A Star Is Born*, *Superman* and *All the President's Men* literally created a new one. So many people wanted to see these pictures immediately that hundreds of theatres were needed to handle the crowds of both curious and serious moviegoers. The box-office sensation created by *President's Men's* release helped its producers to overlook the fact that the film had gone a month over schedule and several million dollars over budget, largely due to Dustin's proclivity for retakes. While Redford had quietly developed his character as the story unfolded, Dustin had insisted on experimenting with scenes and discussing them with anyone who'd listen. This acting approach was costly and time-consuming but of vital importance to Dustin. Happily the end results proved worth the cost.

Many had predicted that the film would fail because the American people wanted to *forget* Watergate, not pay money to see it at the movies, but the general public disagreed and the film chalked up some $30 million during its release.

The potency of the two stars, plus the fine support given them by such actors as Jason Robards Jr., Jack Warden, Jane Alexander and Martin Balsam, added up to some pretty sensational reviews, with many commenting on how Dustin and Redford were able to submerge their individual personalities into their characters. Redford showed an uncanny knack at adapting Woodward's physical mannerisms, journalist-casual dress and halting speech patterns, while Dustin imbued his Bernstein with a true reporter's urgency, all impatience, bluff and bravado as he tracks down leads to the Watergate story.

Some reviewers did quibble about the rightness of Redford and Hoffman for the picture, with *Newsweek's* Jack Kroll saying Dustin 'became a clownish mixture of cajolery and clumsiness', while *The Nation* went so far as to state that the pair were 'too recogniz-able . . . to lure the most gullible of viewers into belief that what they are seeing is the real thing'. But others, including the hard-to-please Rex Reed, disagreed. Reed was frankly in awe of the way they'd managed to submerge their superstar images 'to literally become the reporters they are playing.'

Dustin was pleased when he saw the completed film but was far from enthusiastic about it. The movie's docu-drama style seemed overdone to him but its overall message was, he thought, intact. 'In my opinion, the film is a little too smooth. I would have left a few hairs on the lens. Instead, the film is really a landmark inasmuch as it's the first movie that really said anything even half-assedly true about the Press. Bob deserves this success. Not to take anything away from Alan Pakula, who directed it, but this was Redford's project all the way. He may be the hardest-working actor I've ever known'—no small praise coming from Hoffman!

The film went on to gather eight Oscar nominations, though none for either star. It won a couple of technical awards and, ironically considering all the rewrites and publicity, a Screenwriting Oscar for William Goldman!

Earlier in the year Dustin had voiced some of his feelings about the Academy Awards system, and some people thought his speaking out kept him from another nomination, but one doubts if that was really the case. George C. Scott's big mouth hadn't kept him from winning for *Patton*, and 1976 had been a banner year for actors. Both William Holden and the late Peter Finch had been nominated for the controversial *Network*, joined by Sylvester Stallone's *Rocky*, Robert De Niro's *Taxi Driver* and Giancarlo Giannini's bold acting job in *Seven Beauties*. If anything, the Academy proved it had a heart that year when it gave its first posthumous Best Actor award to the dead Finch for his blistering portrayal of *Network's* alcoholic news messiah. No one felt that award misplaced either, including Dustin, who'd long recognized Finch for the artist he'd been in life and would remain in death thanks to his many films.

# 11

## The matinee idols vs. the ego

In the old studio contract days, movie stars took on pictures for several reasons, the most important being the usage of their contracted commercial talents. Thus Judy Garland would sing her heart out and Betty Hutton would dance her feet off while Jane Powell would try her best to do both. When the front office moguls decreed it, Kathryn Grayson would cinch in her bust and hit an MGM high C in the best Jeanette MacDonald tradition, just as Hedy Lamarr would raise an eyebrow in glamorous close-up to knock moviegoers for a loop.

The male stars did pretty much the same thing, reworking their established screen images in film after film. Gable would be manly no matter what the storyline, Flynn would be properly heroic whether in tights as Robin Hood or in uniform fighting World War II, while Alan Ladd always stood strong, if not tall, in the Western arena.

By the time Dustin Hoffman became a movie star, the contract system was a thing of the distant past. True, there were still a few actors, Robert Redford for example, who pretty much held to their established images as diversions from that path which had most often proved unsuccessful. (More recently, does anyone *really* remember Sly Stallone in *F.I.S.T.* or *Victory*? Probably not, because without his *Rocky* boxing trunks he wasn't able to attract much of an audience.) For Dustin, though, this kind of type-casting had never been a problem because, in the mind of the moviegoer, he was never the same person twice. In fact, up to and including *All the President's Men*, the closest he'd come to playing a conventional male lead was in the comedy *John and Mary* eight years before. Though offered many roles, particularly movie-bios of Gorgeous George, the famous television wrestler, and Willy Sutton, the notorious bank-robber, Dustin wasn't interested. After just playing Lenny Bruce and then Carl Bernstein, he wanted a fictional, 'normal' character to play for a change.

Closing in on his fortieth birthday, Dustin was in a singular

85

position to examine both career and life in general. Career-wise he was in great shape, but personally there were problems. Anne's voicing of her interest in a real acting career of her own was a source of dismay to Dustin. The product of a well-ordered Jewish family relationship, Dustin was basically an old-fashioned man who was perfectly pleased with a mate who stayed home, took care of his children and kept a low profile. As he edged into the timespan of mid-life crisis, he found his personal expectations being questioned, not to mention his self-esteem. The only area where he did have complete control was his career and before it was too late Dustin wanted to play a 'leading man' role. He was certainly ready for it.

Despite the script squabbles on the set of *President's Men*, he had built up a friendly rapport with screenwriter William Goldman, and he was especially taken with a novel Goldman had written in 1974, a tale of international intrigue entitled *The Marathon Man*. The title character, Babe Levy, is a college student living in a rundown section of upper Manhattan whose main refuge from life and the grimness of his surroundings is running around the Central Park Reservoir. The part was a physically demanding one but Dustin liked that aspect of it, particularly since he'd be able to use his own skills as a high school runner in it. He had never been in better shape and wanted a role that would get that across to audiences. *Marathon Man* was it.

As he grew older, Dustin became increasingly better-looking. Now, just shy of forty, his body was tight and trimly well-muscled; with his hair fashionably long (though happily much shorter than his Bernstein bob in *President's Men)*, his angular face came close to being handsome. These were all ingredients he planned on using to bring Babe Levy to onscreen life, and, coupled with the character, made for an exciting prospect.

Another reason Dustin wanted to play the *Marathon Man* was because, for the first time in several pictures, there was a true element of surprise to his character. In *Lenny* the audience went in knowing that, no matter how well performed, the basic story of Lenny Bruce was all downhill, just as in *President's Men* Carl Bernstein's story was uphill. In *Marathon Man* he saw an opportunity to let his admirers just sit back and watch him be manipulated through a story of great suspense, not knowing for certain how it would all come out.

The story itself was a juicy amalgam of murder, torture, intrigue and a pile of diamonds. Though murky at times in its plot it nonetheless moved along with the slapdash speed of a Saturday after-noon serial as an adventure with the good guys and the baddies clearly defined. There was even a mystery woman tossed in for good measure played by the exquisitely European Marthe Keller in her bid for an American movie career; after two tries, she settled for being Al Pacino's live-in lover. Goldman admits he wrote at least four different drafts of a screenplay before the producers were satisfied.

As the film opens, Dustin's character, Babe, is out running and, in the distance, sees the flames of an auto accident. Shortly afterwards, his mysterious older brother shows up and after a restless reunion, during which he voices suspicions of Babe's lady-friend, the exotic Elsa, he winds up dying in his brother's arms, murdered by enemies who suspect he's told his younger brother about his activities as a spy and troubleshooter. These enemies are headed up by an ageing former Nazi leader on whose trail he had been.

Naturally Babe is horrified at his brother's death, but true terror shortly sets in when the Nazi and his minions try to murder him to keep him quiet, while Szell, the Nazi, tries to get to a bank to retrieve a cache of diamonds which represents the fortune he'd stolen from his concentration camp victims. Ironically, it was Szell's brother in the car crash that Babe observed during his run, a man who'd been Szell's New York connection until his death which forces Szell out of his South American refuge and back to New York for the diamonds. One climax follows another, setting off a chain reaction that continues to overturn Babe's life as he tries to save it.

Szell, the Nazi, was formerly a dentist and an expert at torture, both of which talents he uses as he unpacks his tools and drill to extract from Babe the information he *thinks* he knows. Even now, in the days of the slasher movies, these scenes are among the most horrifying ever filmed. Just the sound of the drill as it approaches Babe's vulnerable mouth are enough to set one squirming. When the drill hits his raw teeth, every dentist-chair horror fantasy comes true and it's difficult to stay in your seat.

The centre of both Szell and Babe's story was New York City, so the decision was made to shoot the picture there on location— New York was rapidly becoming Dustin's personal soundstage. That pleased him, as he'd be near his family, but what pleased him even more was John Schlesinger had been signed to direct the film. After *Midnight Cowboy*, Schlesinger had let people know how much he liked Dustin, not only as an actor that he'd directed but also as one of the finest talents in the entire movie business as well. Schlesinger was a director Dustin could trust, and also one he knew would do him well.

Schlesinger began living up to Dustin's expectations when he started assembling a first-rate cast of actors to support him. Roy Scheider, red hot off his *Jaws* success, was set to play the older brother, Doc, while Marthe Keller was cast as the mysterious Elsa and William Devane came on board as Janeway, Doc's confederate in espionage. All that remained to be cast was that pivotal role of Szell, nicknamed in the script 'the White Angel' because of his full mane of white hair.

It was a great part for a scenery-chewing actor, and the producers talked to several character stars before thinking (albeit wistfully) of Sir Laurence Olivier. When they heard he was both interested *and* available, they were delighted. Schlesinger flew to London to meet with Olivier to discuss it, finding an old and fragile man whom he doubted would be able to meet the demands of the part, let alone pass the physical necessary for insurance purposes. Happily, Olivier passed the test and was signed to join the *Marathon Man* cast with rehearsals starting shortly in New York.

Dustin was both thrilled and awed at the opportunity to share the screen with arguably the world's finest actor, but that didn't alter his own ideas about movie-acting, something Olivier would later learn. Before serious rehearsals began, though, there was one particularly delicate problem to be handled which didn't involve Dustin at all. In his book *Adventures in the Screen Trade*, Goldman tells how, since Sir Larry's character was constantly referred to as 'the White Angel' because of his hair, part of the plot necessitated him showing up in New York City bald to avoid any possible chance of his attracting attention to himself. Now Olivier had just been through a series of critical illnesses including cancer of the prostrate, and no one in the company wanted to bring up the possibly touchy subject of his having his head shaved. After all, this was a great actor, a former matinée idol and, perhaps most importantly, an artist who anxiously pursued his craft at every opportunity. If people saw him bald, they'd immediately think his health was even worse than might be suspected, and no one would ever hire him again! A barber was on call but the producers kept him out of sight while they tried to figure out just how to handle this delicate situation. No one wanted to bring it up to

Olivier, thinking that it might upset his already shaky equilibrium. The minutes ticked by while assorted people tried to think how to handle this, but there were no volunteers. Finally, when Olivier appeared on the scene, blood pressures really soared until the actor simply stepped forward and said, 'Would it be possible for me to be shaved bald now? I think it might be best to get it done.' Olivier's lack of personal vanity, especially considering his legendary good looks, proved another valuable asset to the picture.

When Olivier and Dustin began rehearsing together, Dustin, naturally, was anxious to do his best work. Unfortunately for Olivier, though, his best work was often the result of extensive improvisation during rehearsal, making up his lines and emotions as the scene progressed. It was a proven technique for Dustin and, despite any trepidation he might be having at working with such a legendary heavyweight, he wasn't about to change. Olivier knew nothing of this technique, born and raised, as he was, on the beauty of the written, *established* word. When Dustin said, 'Let's put it [the scene] on its feet and improvise,' Olivier was dumbstruck: 'Dear boy, I don't improvise. I wish I did. But I don't.' It was then that he got a lesson in movie-star billing. Dustin's name was to carry the picture, and if Dustin wanted to improvise, that's exactly what would happen. John Schlesinger did not demur, stepping in only to say that, since they were there to rehearse, why not give it a try?

Thus began a long day of exasperation and frustration for Goldman as he watched the frail Olivier try to keep on his feet as Dustin walked him endlessly through a scene. The scene was the most important the two would play together, an underground showdown over the stolen diamonds, but it was also one which came at the end of the film and wasn't scheduled to be shot for months. One would like to rationalize and forgive Dustin's behaviour but, in light of the facts, it's difficult. He undoubtedly knew of Olivier's physical condition and, certainly, there was no pressing need to get involved with that particular scene but Dustin had to actually know that, despite Olivier's golden repu-tation, *he* was the star now. And It took Olivier's painfully swollen ankles to prove it. He never complained, though, probably realizing the futility of it, and proceeded walking most of the afternoon, never once asking for a respite. When he literally limped home after that first rehearsal, he'd earned the respect of everyone, including Dustin.

It's obvious that Dustin has agonized over this episode for years, seeing it for the basically juvenile act it was, as later he amended his recollections of *Marathon Man*. Late in 1984 he made a personal appearance at a theatre where he'd worked as a struggling actor, the Whole Theatre in Montclair, New Jersey, where the subject of Olivier came up. 'He's like a general,' he said, 'very strict. I didn't argue with him [about improvising]. Instead, I said to him, "Tell me what you want me to do".' Dustin's personal re-write might have been triggered by a recent London visit where he ran into the actor at a theatre where his wife, Joan Plowright, was starring in a revival of *The Three Sisters*. 'I saw him, an old man, hardly able to get up the stairs. Nobody helped him and not one of all those English people around him recognized him, one of their greatest actors! I went over to him and said "Hi Lordish," my private nickname for him. He looked up and said, "Dear boy!" '

*Marathon Man* cost $3 million and was finished swiftly enough to come out late in '76, complete with an 8 October première at Hollywood's fabled Mann's Chinese Theatre (formerly Grauman's). Opening box-office figures were very good but the critics were hard put to determine the worthiness of the film, one referring to it as 'a disjointed jigsaw puzzle minus all the pieces'. True, it was a complex attention-needed story but it was far from being, as another critic labelled it, 'the disappointment of the year'. Dustin's work, though, was generally praised. Newsweek said, simply, that he was 'excellent', with Judith Crist adding that his characterization of Babe Levy 'is perfection for the young man'. Also, to Dustin's delight, several important writers mentioned that he'd never looked more fit or more attractive onscreen, assuaging some personal doubts he'd been carrying.

Olivier's work was also praised, to no one's surprise, and the pairing of the old establishment matinée idol with the screen's number-one maverick star was called a highly effective and successful coupling. Veteran critic Arthur Knight called *Marathon Man* 'superior film-making, period', adding that he thought it 'brilliant and disturbing'.

Sadly the film quickly proved not to be the box-office winner that everyone had expected, with its eventual gross only about $8 million. Over the years, though, it's proven to be a steady ratings-grabber on television and, to many, is considered to be one of Dustin's finest films. Seen now, the complicated story makes more sense, when television commercials interrupt its breathless pace for two minutes of much-needed relaxation.

Dustin was keenly disappointed at the borderline acceptance of *Marathon Man*, concluding that the public seemed to like him best playing character parts like Ratso Rizzo and Jack Crabb. He had to swallow the bitter pill that he would never enjoy being a classic movie leading man, but, at the same time, he became determined to advance his career even further by gathering as much control over future projects as possible. There was one story in particular that he'd been working on sporadically for five years and now seemed the perfect time to make it go. He decided that he'd use the first of his two commitments to First Artists to make it, an arrangement where he was guaranteed complete power. In fact, he'd first optioned this particular property back in 1972 just after signing with First Artists.

Based on Edward Bunker's novel *No Beast So Fierce*, the story was a hardhitting look at the struggles of an ex-convict who's trying to make it in the world outside prison walls and still adhere to the strict rules of the parole system. Besides having a large input in writing the script, and starring in it, Dustin decided to take another giant step by directing the film as well. Once the decision was made, he threw himself into preparing the film with an almost frightening totality. For months he visited various prisons both in Los Angeles and around the country, even getting himself behind the walls of San Francisco's San Quentin. In LA he went to the county jail and went through the procedure of being arrested just as in real life: fingerprints, mug shots, the works. As a joke, one of the officers ran Dustin's name though the police computer but the results weren't funny when it popped up because of two unpaid traffic tickets. A red-faced Dustin quietly paid the overdue fines and left.

After choosing locations at California's Folsom Prison and in and around LA, Dustin scheduled production to begin in mid-march of 1977. Rewrites on the script continued right up to the starting date as various writers aided him in getting together the story of Max Dembo. Certainly Dustin had played sleazy characters before, but even Ratso Rizzo shone besides this one. The book's author was himself an ex-con, so the character of Max was mired in truth about how the prison system and its aftermath could affect a loser like him.

The movie, now titled *Straight Time*, began shooting under a haze of controlled optimism and healthy expectations. First Artists seemed delighted at Dustin's choosing double duty as both star and director, and they were pleased with the variety of

91

respected actors he'd chosen to support him, a group that included Harry Dean Stanton, Gary Busey, Bonnie Bedelia and Clarence Williams Jr., the black actor who first won fame on televisions *Mod Squad* and, more recently, played Prince's father in 1984's *Purple Rain*. All critically appreciated actors, they were eager to participate in Dustin's directorial debut, but the proper actor-director chemistry just simply wasn't there.

After several weeks of shooting, the film's budget was heavily dented, with literally nothing screenable to show for it. Dustin was in a state of shock, feeling he'd worked sufficiently long and well over his career to handle this double assignment. Literally thousands of his scarce personal hours had gone into the preparation for this picture, and he had desperately wanted it to work, now especially after the disappointment of *Marathon Man*.

Right in the middle of this turmoil, and only serving to make matters even more emotionally cloudy for Dustin, was the fact that his wife had finally got another acting job. On her own, Anne had auditioned for Italian director Lina Wertmuller for a new comedy called *It Never Rains but it Pours*. She had been studying acting intensively for the past year, and her dogged determination paid off when Wertmuller cast her to play Candice Bergen's friend. Though, admittedly, she couldn't command much of a salary, Anne felt this would be the opening she'd been looking for to express her own talent. Also, considering the film would be Wertmuller's first American–financed, English-speaking production, there would be a built-in international audience of cinema critics and heavyweights, any of whom might be smart enough to spot Anne Byrne as the star material she thought she was.

Wertmuller had made a splashy name for herself in 1977 when her *Seven Beauties* opened in New York City, finding herself hailed as the latest saviour of the dormant Italian film industry. The following year, with her next film, *Swept Away*, she was even more heralded and Warner Brothers decided her talent was bankable enough for them to finance her first American film, to be shot on location in Italy and San Francisco. Somehow, though, Wertmuller's constant cinematic lecture on the battle of the sexes didn't translate into English. Besides her own 'star', Giancarlo Giannini of both *Seven Beauties* and *Swept Away*, she added Candice Bergen, an actress just on the brink of her best work. Too bad for Wertmuller that Bergen was to hit the brink two years later with *Starting Over*, because she obviously did not do so in what turned into a major, and quickly forgettable, disappointment, redubbed

*The End of the World in our Bed in a Night Full of Rain.*

Released early in 1978, the misnamed comedy of an American feminist (Bergen) and the Italian chauvinist Communist (Giannini) caused few sparks with moviegoers, grossing less than $1 million in its initial, and spotty, release. Anne's part was expectedly small (she was billed seventh in the cast) and, while well done, did not elevate her into instant stardom or an independent career. There would be more parts, such as that of Tony Roberts' wife in Woody Allen's *Manhattan* and, in 1980, a co-starring role opposite Treat Williams in *Why Would I Lie?* but by then she was the *ex*-Mrs Dustin Hoffman. During the *Straight Time* period, though, she was still very much his wife, even though the marriage seemed headed directly towards the proverbial rocks.

Dustin's preoccupation with the film wasn't helping that from happening, and his occasional complaints over Anne's search for individuality only strengthened her resolve to succeed. It was all too obvious that something had to give. During *Straight Time* production Dustin had to spend many nights away from home, and shortly the tabloid rumour-mills had the couple split. He told reporters that his nights away were only because of the stress of filming and that he returned to the nest every weekend—all well and good, but once the rumours had started, even those closest to the couple couldn't truthfully deny them.

Besieged by both personal and professional problems, Dustin reached out to his old friend Ulu Grosbard for help, asking him to take over the direction of *Straight Time.* Despite his personal desire to star and direct, Dustin was smart enough to realize that he wouldn't be able to pull it off. As one of the producers of the film, it was Dustin-the-executive who made the decision to let Dustin-the-director go. Grosbard realized how deeply this setback affected his friend, and only grudgingly agreed to take over. Any premonition Grosbard might have had about doing so shortly proved to be correct. As the former director, Dustin had reached such a stage of mental preparedness that it was virtually impossible for him to accept someone else—even a dear friend—and thus began the last association of what had been a long and happy friendship.

When Grosbard directed Dustin in *Who is Harry Kellerman . . . ?* years earlier, he'd learned first-hand about his temperament. Now he saw it again, magnified by both Dustin's steady years of stardom and his borderline obsession with this particular project. After working on the story for years and visualizing it in his mind,

Dustin wasn't prepared to deal with any 'new' director—even if he was an old and supposedly trusted friend. Almost immediately, Grosbard realized he'd signed himself into a no-win situation, but to fulfil his duties he risked the wrath of his star and friend because his reputation as a director had to take precedence over any personal feelings.

Filming resumed in September '77, and whatever dreams either man had of a triumphant collaboration were quickly scotched as arguments over Dustin's characterization became commonplace. A clash of egos? Certainly. A clash of talents equally committed? One wonders. In fact, the only thing anyone was certain of was that things were not going well.

First Artists remained cautiously anxious about the film. It was, after all, Dustin's first picture for them. Their reservations grew, however, when the shooting schedule of sixty-one days ran over by some two weeks, with no end in sight and both Hoffman and Grosbard unhappy with most of the footage that had been shot. By then Dustin was signed for a second film with First Artists, *Agatha*, and time was running out between the completion date of *Straight Time* and the starting date of *Agatha*. When a First Artists executive suggested a hiatus in production to give Dustin and Grosbard time to assemble their footage, review it and then set up a new schedule to finish the film, Dustin agreed. Ready to leave for Britain where *Agatha* was to be shot, he decided that a break in the seemingly endless problems of *Straight Time* made perfect sense. It was only much later, in Britain, that he was informed that *Straight Time* was finished as far as First Artists was concerned, and shortly the company exercised their right to take the film and edit it themselves. Naturally Dustin was appalled. Not only had he traded his million-dollar salary for artistic control of the picture but, in his heart, he knew he'd also sacrificed a friend to it. Had he had any idea of what First Artists was planning, he would never have agreed to the friendly offer of a hiatus.

Technically First Artists did have a case, what with *Straight Time's* being both overschedule and over budget, but Dustin never believed they'd resort to using it. The only portion that he was pleased with was some twenty-odd minutes that he'd edited as filming went along, but it had been enough to make him think that, after the hiatus, he and Grosbard could put the pieces together into something they'd be proud of. It was a gamble he was looking forward to as he was beginning to understand that the real magic of making movies happened in the editing room. Now he had to surrender all his power on *Straight Time* and go right into a new film which, on first glance, seemed as unorganized as the one he was leaving behind. Dustin's first film for First Artists was turning into a disaster, and he was further incensed when one executive let it be known that the company had wrapped *Straight Time* because the whole production was 'out of control'.

Dustin was positive that, despite the many problems, his acting in *Straight Time* was some of his best ever, and was further distraught that it was now lost to him. 'I was doing the best work I'd ever done,' he later said, 'and I knew the film wasn't supporting the performance.' When Grosbard heard this, he replied, 'If he's so meticulous and such a perfectionist, why had he created such an enormous mess?' In short, the friendship was over, and further verbal brickbats were only added nails in its coffin.

# 12

## *Agatha* and the end of a marriage

*Agatha* started out as a 'little picture' with a fanciful explanation of the eleven-day disappearance of novelist Agatha Christie in December 1926. As originally conceived, it was to be a vehicle for two female stars, one playing Christie and the other her husband's mistress. Once its producers, First Artists, were able to interest Dustin in it, though, the story had to be retailored to include his talents, and in a very short period of time. When Dustin had first read the script, which would star Vanessa Redgrave as Agatha Christie, his part was small but vivid and he was perfectly willing to act what was virtually a cameo. First Artists quickly had other ideas, wanting their male star to *star*, and said as much to screenwriter Kathleen Tynan. Commented Tynan later, 'When I wrote the part of the journalist, he was a tall, blond Englishman with a supporting role. Now, he's a small, dark American with one of the leads.' The revised script was not finished when Dustin showed up in London to begin work. As was getting to be a most unwelcome habit, he started the film without a finished scenario. He later offered, 'I literally got on my knees and begged them not to start the film. Once you go on the floor to make a movie, it's crazy time. It's painting a picture on railroad tracks, with the train getting closer. *Agatha* was every actor's nightmare. The script was literally being rewritten every day.'

Dustin found it virtually impossible to do any satisfying work when pages were thrust at him just before shooting, and at one point his fiery co-star, Redgrave, simply refused to go ahead until she'd had a chance to study and rehearse her script fully. When the company took a Christmas break, it was a blessing for all concerned. The writers would have time to work in peace, while Redgrave would have the same to cool down.

It proved to be no vacation for Dustin, though, because, instead of heading home to New York and family for the holidays, he flew to Los Angeles to continue trying to edit a rough cut of *Straight*

*Time.* Despite the fact that First Artists had shut down the picture in July, Dustin contractually had six months to deliver a rough cut and had been so determined to do so that segments of the film had been shipped to Britain so he could work on it during the making of *Agatha.* This trip was his last chance to finish it, but even working night and day he had to return to *Agatha* with only about one quarter of *Straight Time* edited to his satisfaction.

Back in Britain, production resumed on *Agatha* but only briefly before First Artists issued an ultimatum that they cease filming immediately. By then it *was* virtually finished but not to Dustin's satisfaction. He argued that he needed more time for an additional scene which, to him, would make the complicated story of Agatha and the reporter who traces her after her disappearance believable. First Artists said no, shooting stopped, and Dustin didn't get his scene. In retrospect, he was absolutely right this time, for in the finished film one never does realize or understand just why his character of a London gossip columnist is so obsessed with Mrs Christie. Had they included the extra small scene in which he confesses to her that he's a failed novelist who'd grown to admire her for her success in that genre of writing, the focal point of their relationship would have made perfect sense. As it is, and despite its beautiful sepia-toned photography and elegant production values, his interest in finding Agatha seems primarily that of just another dedicated reporter tracking down a scoop.

So adamant was Dustin about the importance of this scene that he offered to pay for an extra day's shooting to film it. First Artists turned him down cold. At this point, after reluctantly walking away from *Agatha,* he tried going back again to work on the editing of *Straight Time,* only to find out it had been totally removed from his hands and that First Artists would edit the release print.

Dustin's sense of professional impotence reached a new high, so much so that he refused to complete the dubbing of *Agatha* unless he got *Straight Time* back. First Artists began raising their legal voices, but before they had time to get serious, he reconsidered and finished the dubbing. He realized that if he didn't, another actor's voice would be patched in and the picture would wind up being even worse than he thought it was already. Also, despite his feelings for the film, he realized his obligation to the people who'd be buying tickets to see him.

With these two experiences behind him, Dustin could only take heart that they concluded his two-picture contract with the company. Founded in such a blaze of creative optimism, over its few years life First Artists was proving a major disappointment to all its member stars, particularly Dustin. He felt compromised and he didn't like it. As had happened before, he felt he'd been promised the moon only to end up with a gnawing sense of dissatisfaction and disillusion. Feeling justified, he ended February '78 by filing a huge lawsuit against First Artists. In the $30 million-plus legal action, he accused First Artists of seizing creative control over the two films, *Straight Time* and *Agatha*, for which he'd sacrificed most of his $2 million salary. He wanted that money plus many millions more in damages for breach of contract, and $3 million more in exemplary damages against First Artists' president and Jarvis Astaire his own business manager.

Dustin tried to stop Warner Brothers from releasing *Agatha* but lost that round. Warners also released *Straight Time* in March '78 but did so under a veritable cloud of secrecy. It opened on a Friday with no advance screenings for the Press, which was, and is, a sure sign that the studio had no faith in the picture to begin with, hoping to get a good weekend's business before the reviews came out about just how bad it was.

The entire First Artists venture was a fiasco as far as Dustin was concerned. In the end, the exectives looking for fast money had won out over the group of actors dedicated first and foremost to doing a good and secure job. It was a lesson he never forgot, nor failed to use in the future. 'I had the shit kicked out of me, and that can be very valuable in going through life. I learned not to trust anybody.'

Critical and public reception to both these films was mixed, with Dustin's usual patrons on his side while others, like Pauline Kael, did their expected hatchet jobs. For once, Dustin couldn't disagree. *Straight Time*, the dream project to make him respected not just as an actor but as a director too, was an embarrassment to him. This was an opinion he formed then, and nothing would change his mind even when *Straight Time* was lauded as a gritty, almost-documentary slice of raw life and earned a place on several Ten Best Films of the Year lists. Somehow he couldn't accept the picture as being any good without its having the particular stamp on it he'd envisioned for close to six years.

As late as 1979, with no end in sight to his complicated lawsuit, he remained optimistic that he'd eventually get the film back and finally be able to edit his own version. When asked about the lawsuit, he'd quickly change the subject back to *Straight Time*. 'It looks like I'm going to get my film back and I'll be able to recut it and send it out the way I wanted to from the first.' Perhaps a clue to Dustin's obsession with the film was the way the character of Max Dembo possessed him: 'My role as the ex-con was the most difficult I've ever done. It was the hardest to shake, too. I just couldn't get him out of my system. [After filming] I shaved off the beard I grew for the part and scrubbed my face but he stayed with me. I just couldn't get that grimy feeling off.'

*Agatha*, filmed in sepia-toned Technicolor, was a beautiful, stylish film to look at, and critics raved about Redgrave's lustrous performance as Mrs Christie, the emotionally disabled wife who hatches an elaborate plot to thwart her husband's mistress, only to be saved by American-born 'gossip columnist' Wally Stanton. As Wally, Dustin got a few good reviews himself, including the *Saturday Review's* nod that he 'conveys a marvellous sensitivity beneath an air of acquired confidence'. Leave it to Pauline Kael, though, to see the seams in the plot: 'Wally Stanton is just a concoction of a role,' she snorted, adding that he was 'furiously theatrical' in playing it.

Considering Dustin's difficulty in ridding himself of Max Dembo, plus the protracted stress of *Straight Time*, it's a wonder he could play such a totally reverse character at all in such a short time, but he does, and with a slick style and believability. He brings an almost courtly charm to his role, even making his shortness work effectively against Redgrave's towering, fur-bedecked Mrs Christie.

Ironically, one of the actors who came out best from the experience was Timothy Dalton, then Redgrave's off-screen lover. As Colonal Archie Christie, the classically handsome actor gave a startling impersonation of a young Sir Laurence Olivier. The Redgrave/Dalton affair was even then several years old, and he obviously relished having a part where he could spurn his lover, talk horribly to her and yet see her continue to be consumed with love for him. Unfortunately the film did little to boost him to the international stardom of which his talent seemed worthy.

Redgrave's Christie continued to be praised, with many commenting that the role was the kind of vaguely romantic, vulnerable character in which she excelled. *Films In Review* called *Agatha* 'a perfect Sunday afternoon diversion . . . film to take Mom and Dad to. You might leave the film unprovoked, maybe half-asleep, but you won't feel cheated.'

Neither picture was the success it should have been. After less than four full months of release, Warner brothers took *Straight Time* out of circulation after adding up a meagre box-office total of only $4 million. Considering the budget ended up topping 3.5 million, the film was an unmitigated flop. As for *Agatha*, It just never found its audience.

As '79 approached, Dustin had reason to look back over the past decade. He had started it with such enthusiasm and optimism and now it was ending in disappointment, frustration and misdirection of ambitious talent. Of the nine films he'd made during the seventies, only two, *Papillon* and *All The President's Men*, had been popular successes. The bad publicity, deserved or not, over the two First Artists films had pinpointed Dustin as a temperamental star in Hollywood's eyes—and, worse yet, a temperamental star who wasn't a guaranteed moneymaker! Grosbard had called him 'a professional victim' for his tantrums on *Straight Time*, and there were many who believed him.

That picture is pivotal in Dustin's life for several reasons already mentioned but certainly not the least of them was the separation it caused with his family. He established a California base by leasing a house in Westwood during the filming and spent most weekends there, conspicuously absent in New York. At first Dustin blamed it on the personality immersion he'd undergone as Max Dembo and his subsequent inability to set the ugly character aside after work, but stories began making the Press that all his off-hours weren't being spent quietly at home and that something was seriously amiss with the Hoffman marriage.

Anne still had high hopes for her own acting career even after the fiasco of the Wertmuller movie, and her patience with tending her husband's forty-one-year-old ego was wearing increasingly thin. After all, he was a superstar while she was still struggling for a professional identity. Also he was used to getting just about everything he wanted by sheer force of personality. (Back in 1975, when casting *All Over Town*, Dustin had interviewed Polly Holliday for a part. She got it and, later, was consoled by Dustin at its early closing. He told her, 'I'll see you in Hollywood. You'll end up there because you're just as mean as I am.' A year later he gave her a small part in *President's Men* and then came television's *Alice*. Toughness, according to Dustin, not only could but *did* pay off!)

Actually it wasn't a natural toughness that had been seeing him through his recent career swings but an acquired one, a learned sense of survival that precluded outside interference. It had taken him so long to circumvent his childhood hang-ups and now that he seemed finally able to handle that, he wasn't young enough any more to enjoy a liberated youth. He was verging on middle age and was now caught deeply in its crisis. And this was a man who still worried about his skin, going often to New York cosmetician Lia Shorr to have his face massaged—because 'He loves to be pampered' but most importantly because 'When he's into a part he breaks out from stress.'

For Dustin, the stress was yet to come!

Incongruously, it was at this time that he was approached about a new picture, the story of a divorce and its aftermath called *Kramer vs. Kramer*. Initially he turned the script down as being too simplistic and treacly, and writer/director Robert Benton proceeded to shop it around to several other actors, including George Hamilton. Benton's mind, though, kept returning to Dustin and, after rewriting the script, he again contacted him. Again Dustin resisted until Benton offered to let him help reshape the screenplay into something closer to what he wanted, during a work period that would last some eight months.

It was during this stage of preparing *Kramer vs. Kramer* that Dustin's life and art came together again when Anne decided to divorce him. She cited 'mutual reasons' for the split and, since then, neiter she nor Dustin has expanded much on that. The most logical assumption is that his career and its strains plus her stifled ambition combined to make for an unhappy and unfulfilling marriage. After ten years, it was all over bar the shouting. Dustin admitted it was largely his fault, stating, 'You can't have a career and a family. Film-making is set up so that you don't have enough time. My family suffered.' Dodging specifics, he shortly added that, 'The reasons are personal and complicated, as I'm sure they are for anyone else in this situation. Most separations come from the basic reason: something is structurally wrong in the beginning.'

Anne had once commented that, above anything else, Dustin 'demands honesty. Dusty really believes your most important thing is to be what you are. That's very wonderful. And *very* difficult.' Certainly it was also very difficult to make the decision to end the marriage, but at least Anne had been honest in doing so.

As for Dustin, he didn't disguise the fact that he could be hard to deal with whether he was working or not! 'But when I am working, I'm just unable to function in any kind of normal way when I get home. It's not so much that I'm taking home the character as I'm taking home the disappointment, the fatigue. It's draining

101

working thirteen to fourteen hours at a stretch, doing maybe a two-minute scene.' Sadly, to those closest to him, it seemed that when his career came into conflict with his personal life, it was the career that came out on top.

Much later Dustin was able to tell *Ladies' Home Journal* more about the personal conflicts that resulted from his splintered attentions. 'Anne and I thought our fighting was healthy in a sense, even all the *Who's Afraid of Virginia Woolf* scenes, and we used to brag we weren't like those people who say "We never fight." But I guess you just can't battle that much over a number of years without ultimately—you know.' He reiterated that, when a marriage goes wrong, it was usually wrong from the beginning, 'something structurally unsound and there were signs you didn't pay attention to'. He continued: 'The reason for our divorce had to do with differing viewpoints, and I don't think it would have workaholic ad-agency executive who comes home one evening wounds of the divorce, which was lengthy, argumentative and very expensive, had been salved by his happy remarriage, but at the time he was very shaken.

All his personal sorrows, frustrations and emotional reactions to his situation were channelled into the character of Ted Kramer, a workaholic ad-agency exectutive who comes home one evening to hear his wife tell him she's leaving him and their young son to go into the world and 'find her own identity'.

Once it became clear to Dustin that the divorce was a long and noisy reality, he turned, as before, to his work for at least partial solace, using his experiences almost as they happened in a therapeutic attempt to put the pain and disorder of his life into some semblance of rationality. George Hamilton might have once been offered this particular part but it was Dustin Hoffman who could most emotionally relate to it. As with Ted Kramer in the film, Dustin's ideal marriage had ended, and the actor and the man were coming together again.

Alfredo (Dustin) thinks he's just found the girl of his dreams in *Alfredo, Alfredo.* Little does he know what's ahead!

A bewildered and sunglassed Alfredo marries his dream girl (Carla Gravina) while her voracious parents look happily on

Lenny (Dustin Hoffman) reflects a good
audience reaction in *Lenny*

A rare happy moment for Lenny Bruce and his wife, Honey (Dustin and Valerie Perrine) in *Lenny*

Dustin and Robert Redford share a conspiratorial moment as under-cover reporters Bernstein and Woodward in the award-winning *All the President's Men* in 1976. Surprisingly, the egotistic superstars got on well during the extended shooting schedule of the film

Dustin gets into his Carl Bernstein character just before a take on the set of *All the President's Men*. The film's subsequent success helped restore his popularity

Dustin and producer Robert Evans pause for a moment of guarded good humour on the set of 1976's popular *Marathon Man*, considered by many to be one of Dustin's most entertaining films

Babe (Dustin Hoffman) and his exotic Elsa (Marthe Keller) prepare to confront his torturers in *Marathon Man*. Despite a huge publicity build-up, the film failed to make Keller the 'Garbo of the 70s' as had been hoped for

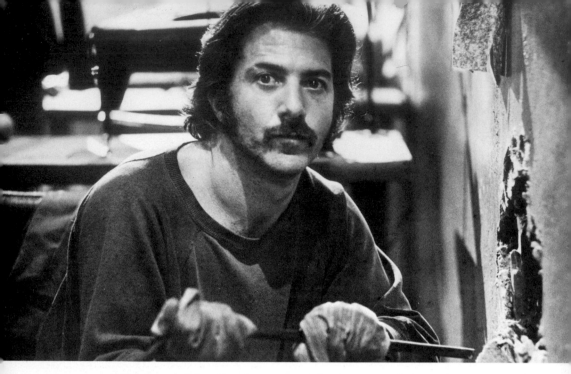

A Desperate Max Dembo in *Straight Time*, the ill-fated film that was to have been Dustin's directorial debut

The missing Agatha Christie (Vanessa Redgrave) unknowingly meets the man who is searching for her (Dustin Hoffman) in *Agatha's* gothic health spa

In *Kramer vs. Kramer*, Dustin plays Ted Kramer, the workaholic advertising executive who pays more attention to his job than to his marriage – and with disastrous results

The explosive, improvised scene in *Kramer vs. Kramer* that helped make the film a gigantic hit and Meryl Streep a major star

Ted Kramer (Dustin Hoffman) and his son (Justin Henry) in a studio portrait from *Kramer vs. Kramer*. The mutual affection is obvious

# 13

## *Kramer vs. Kramer* – life and art combine

Benton's guarantee of Dustin's collaborating on the screenplay of *Kramer vs. Kramer*, along with the film's producer Stanley Jaffe, *and* following through with it, was a lifesaver for Dustin. At last he was able to contribute openly to a film, and the satisfaction helped offset the fact that what he was writing was almost the truth of his real life. The three of them would closet themselves in a hotel room and shut out the world as they went over the screenplay line by line, analysing, questioning and fleshing out each scene for the most dramatic impact. Finally Dustin was in the ideal position, signing a contract that gave him not only a million-dollar salary and a percentage of the profits but also a writer/director who was prepared to deal with him. Benton admitted easily that, 'I attempted to write the way Dustin talks, so that when he improvises [as Benton knew he would!], you wouldn't know the difference. Benton and Jaffe were eager to please Dustin since they knew he was the best actor for the part. They were equally willing to let him be part of the creative force, especially after he'd told them upfront that, 'I want to be a collaborator. Otherwise I'm going back to the theatre.' After his two recent screen disappointments, they did not doubt his seriousness.

Once he'd committed himself to *Kramer vs. Kramer* and knew for sure that there was a concrete professional future, Dustin turned his head to other interests, primarily new women. He'd once told an interviewer his ideal: 'I've [always] been most attracted to women who were working behind counters—salesgirls, waitresses, working girls—rather than rich women who go shopping every day.' Since then, however, he'd expanded his horizons to include successful women who could fully appreciate his lifestyle and all that went with it. One of these was Kate Jackson, the brunette actress then best known as the smartest of television's *Charlie Angels*. She was then just ending a brief marriage to Andrew Stevens and was as footloose as Dustin. The pair started popping up on both coasts as he continued to split his time between Westwood and his New York co-op. At New York's Studio 54 nightclub, photographers cornered them on a night out, with a bearded Dustin looking stoic while flashbulbs popped, and Jackson, a man's shirt pulled over a T-shirt and hair hanging limply down to her shoulders, seemingly trying to push them away. As usual, the papparazzi won and the stars ended up peering uncomfortably out of the tabloids. Those same newspapers were shortly referring to Kate as Dustin's 'constant companion', especially when she began being touted as the actress to play opposite him in *Kramer vs. Kramer*.

In fact, Jackson might well have played the part of Joanna Kramer but ABC had other ideas. The network that produced her mega-hit series *Charlie's Angels* was not about to let her out of her contract to make the film, and a great career opportunity was lost. When the 'angels' finished flying over the airwaves two years later, interest in making Jackson a movie star had noticeably quietened. Her one big chance, the homosexually angled love triangle *Making Love*, released in 1982, was a major flop and to salvage her career she wisely returned to the small screen.

Dustin wasn't ready for any kind of real attachment, though, and was shortly dating other women—lots of them. His mid-life crisis was rapidly turning into a personal carnival, and the adulation he received from the opposite sex, his reward for being a recognized, and now single, sex symbol, was intense. After ten years of marriage, there was a need to make the most of his new-found freedom, but as he neared another birthday some of the fun began going out of it. Instead of being a sexually insecure youth, bedevilled by his big nose and short stature and eager to score anywhere he could, he was now a man past forty, an international movie star who could have any woman he wanted just for the asking. Happily Dustin's dedication to his acting craft matched that of his sexuality, surpassing it now as *Kramer vs. Kramer* got closer to reality.

The film was scheduled to start filming in New York on 12 June 1978, but before that the producers—with Dustin's input and approval—had to find the right actress to play opposite him. Enter a young woman named Meryl Streep.

Once it was clear that Jackson would not be available, they auditioned a great many other actresses for Joanna, stars and newcomers alike. Streep was among the latter, although she had scored well in the television mini-series *Holocaust* and on the New

York stage. She had also made two films, *The Deer Hunter* and *The Secduction of Joe Tynan*, but neither had yet been released, so her wide-screen presence remained an unknown.

Originally Meryl's agent sent her up for the much smaller role of Phyllis, the lady lawyer who, after spending a night with Ted Kramer, unexpectedly bumps into his young son the morning after as she's walking naked through his apartment. And this, indeed, was the part she auditioned for with Dustin, Benton and producer Stanley Jaffe. When it was all over, the three agreed that Meryl was terrific—but not for the smaller part. 'She Joanna!', they exclaimed, forgetting her lack of big screen credits and a box-office name.

As Dustin had been the first of a new breed of leading man, so was Streep a unique leading woman. Not classically beautiful, she nonetheless exuded a haunting quality that combined the mystery of a sixteenth-century Italian painting with a crisp modernity of style that made for a beguiling combination. One wonders if Dustin recognized her as the young actress he'd turned down several years before for *All Over Town*. If he did, he kept it to himself. Meryl might have called him a pig for his copping a feel during their earlier run-in, but now she'd be his wife on film. And now that was the most important, if not only, consideration!

Biographer Diana Maychick has described Meryl's character perfectly when she called Joanna Kramer an 'unhappy woman on the brink of a nervous breakdown she knew would never come': that was completely true. As written, she takes a good deal of getting used to before one can dredge up an iota of sympathy for her. When she abruptly walks out on her husband and son at the beginning of the film, the audience feels a natural resentment against her selfishness that doesn't dissipate until much later in the story. Through Streep's fragile artistry, though, the audience eventually, if begrudgingly, forgives her, so much so that they're left in a bind as to who to root for in the climatic custody trial. (So effective did Streep become in the part that, at one point, screenwriter Benton's wife, Sally, asked him to rewrite the ending to give her custody of their son instead of Dustin!)

As had rarely happened before—except when *The Graduate* met Mrs Robinson, perhaps—Dustin had a female co-star who seriously challenged him. Her reservoir of talent also included a theatrical background which included improvisation, and this was a point that led to problems on the set. Meryl knew that her brief part had to be totally utilized to make her Joanna understandable, and when she felt the script wasn't quite doing the job, she improvised dialogue to make her point.

Now Dustin always considered this technique pretty much his personal territory on a movie, and when Meryl started using it also, he immediately went on the defensive, feeling she'd upstage him. But while he later said that they did indeed have several 'bad fights', the end result was classic cinema.

Perhaps the most well-known example of this infighting was the restaurant scene in which Joanna confronts Ted with her desire to take her son back. It was the perfect example of Meryl feeling she didn't have enough of the right dialogue to establish her character's case. Actually neither star was happy with the dialogue, but when Streep began improvising lines and business, Dustin was flabbergasted and fought back. As written, she was supposed to demand her son at the beginning of the scene, with no emotional build-up. Meryl went to Benton expressing her concern over this and asking if it couldn't come later. He agreed to the change but Dustin didn't. With the cameras rolling, they tried it her way though, and it worked much better. Dustin realized this but also felt bested by Meryl at the scene's end. Unable to strike back verbally, he punctuated his script silence by suddenly smashing a wineglass at the wall between them, and the look of total shock on Meryl's face when this happens is completely real. It was the last thing she was expecting but it made the whole sequence work better for both of them.

Once Dustin realized that Meryl's objections were for the betterment of the picture and not just herself, he re-evaluated his opinion of her, later saying that, 'Yes, I hated her guts [at the time] but I respected her . . . She sticks with her guns and doesn't let anyone mess with her when she thinks she's right.' Benton simply sighed, well out of earshot, that 'Someone as obsessed as Dustin creates a lot of tension and puts a tremendous burden on the people he works with.'

Once Meryl knew she was being taken seriously, she was able to devote herself to her character and re-evaluate *her* opinion of Dustin and his character, Ted Kramer. 'He's the prototypical seventies person and you just can't *stand* him! But Dustin makes him so funny—as a high pressure, real finger-popping, fast-talking guy, somebody who has an answer for everything. He's so un-neurotic in a way, and yet when you see the way he has to make a living, it's horrible.'

As an actress Streep had analysed the mentality of Ted Kramer, the advertising executive who makes his living by his glib tongue and fast action. In reality, that analysis was one she could as easily have made of Dustin himself.

Perhaps the main reason for the ego clashes and misunderstandings between Dustin and Meryl was because they were able to experience a natural progression of their respective feelings about Ted and Joanna. Benton, the director, was shooting the film in sequence. While it was a longer, more difficult and certainly more expensive process, he felt it was necessary so that the tension between the Kramers and their young son could build to a natural climax to get the optimum effect of balance and feeling. It was certainly a gamble on Benton's part, but one he was willing to take. The months of working so closely with Dustin had cemented the feeling in his mind that he'd do his best work if allowed to grow and evolve his character just as the story unfolds. It was a rare opportunity to be able to work this way, and Dustin also appreciated the fact that producer Jaffe never complained about any added cost!

The object of the Kramers' contention, their son Billy, was played by a tiny seven-year-old named Justin Henry, found after a long and tedious search. Benton, Jaffe and often Dustin interviewed some three hundred children before finding him, a process so lengthy and involved that, at one point Dustin wanted to change the sex of the Kramers' child and cast his daughter, Jennifer! When he met little Justin, though, he realized the chemistry was perfect between them and he was signed for the film. Blond and blue-eyed, Justin had never acted before but Dustin knew instinctively that he could do the job. 'I sat through—God, I can't be sure—maybe one hundred or so interviews looking for the right kid . . . I made at least forty video tapes with the best of the kids. I felt that was very important,' he told *Films in Focus*, 'because the young actor who played Billy, my son, had to be absolutely comfortable working with me or the film just wouldn't work. Happily, He liked me. It was crazy about him too—he's such a decent kid. Whatever feelings between us appear on the screen were there off screen as well . . . He and I would discuss a scene and he'd ask me what my kids did, or what I thought they'd do in a similar situation.'

It was obvious that Dustin's children, Jenna, nine, and stepdaughter Karina, thirteen, were much on his mind during the shooting of *Kramer vs. Kramer,* and being in New York enabled him to spend more time with them, an experience that proved

107

thought-provoking and gave him insight. Undeniably he felt a certain guilt about the effect his divorce from Anne was having on them. It was obvious from the start that their loyalties had to be divided. Remembering Dustin's own childhood feelings of alienation from his family and his constant striving to succeed and belong, it's easy to understand his concern. He tried explaining his feelings, saying, 'You kid yourself if you think being separated does not have a traumatic effect on children. They are going to feel that it is somehow expected that they favour one parent over the other, and that causes conflict.'

Dustin truly loved the children and, in fact, was looking forward to someday having more. Now, though, he was only aware of their pain and confusion and tried to make life as normal as possible for them. 'I don't think it's possible to give a child too much love. I try not to spoil mine, because I'm aware that there is a tendency to over-compensate when you're separated.' The visits to his daughters were also serving another purpose as he was forced to recognize and deal with the parallels between his personal life and the screen relationship between Ted Kramer and his child. 'When the girls first visited me, they would test me. Whatever I'd say to do, they'd do just the opposite. Things I knew they always liked, they'd say they didn't like. I couldn't please them. They were testing me, you know, like kids will do when they're angry with the people they love the most. It's so frustrating to a parent. You want to scream, to break their necks—God, you just feel so damned frustrated and mad at them, at yourself, at everyone.' It proved to be useful anger. 'That scene at the dinner table, when Billy says he hates Swiss steaks and defies his father and gets the ice-cream out of the freezer—that came out of something that really happened.'

Eventually Dustin was to make sense of the whole situation: 'It may sound strange but to be experiencing in real life what I was portraying on the screen was for me, as an actor, a pleasure I'd never had.'

Indeed he used *Kramer vs. Kramer* as a life experience as well as an acting challenge, almost practising on his movie child how to handle the problems of his real ones. 'Benton left me alone with Justin to work those feelings into parallel scenes in the script.' and since they were shooting sequentially he could learn day by day how to handle the problems and readjustments that a broken home unwillingly invites into the lives of those involved.

One of the most touching scenes in the film is when Ted agrees to let Joanna see her son again, insisting that this emotional reunion take place in Central Park. Dustin walks along the pathway holding his son's hand as we glimpse a raincoated Joanna waiting anxiously ahead, one hand raised in a plaintive greeting. When Billy recognizes her, he runs into her arms. After the scene was shot and the pressure was off, Dustin asked Justin, 'Who do you really want to live with?', at which point the youngster yelled, 'Her! She's nicer.' The assembled members of the cast and crew laughed at his spontaneous outburst. 'Oh yeah?' countered Dustin. 'Work with her five weeks and then see what you say.' It was a joke made in tribute to his growing understanding of her as a professional. And from Hoffman, it was a compliment both rare and worthwhile. Later he'd add that Meryl would 'work twenty hours a day. She's an ox when it comes to acting. She eats work for breakfast. It's like playing with Billie Jean King. She keeps trying to hit the perfect ball.'

In the famous courtroom scene where she pleads for the return of her son, Meryl improvised again, but this time Dustin was able to appreciate and accept what she was doing. When she, literally, rewrote the speech of why she'd walked out on her family, director Benton's first thought was 'I'm going to lose two days' work. One rewriting what she's done, and the other soothing her feelings.' Not so. Her improvised plea was 'brilliant', and in the finished film, 'What you see up there is hers.' For Dustin's reaction shot, with all the cameras trained on him, she did the scene again with equal intensity. When the crew finished the shot and turned back to her, 'There was Meryl in tears. She'd given that much just for a reaction shot.'

Meanwhile the Press, always looking for a 'juicy Hoffman story', played up his intensity on *Kramer vs. Kramer* in an unflattering light, carping on his 'temperamental' behaviour which included the breathless fact that 'The cast and crew were bending over backwards to placate him' as he 'locks himself in his trailer at lunchtime and stares blankly out of the windows until he is awakened from his trance.' One of the reasons for this behaviour was reported to be that he was depressed because other stars, including old friend Jon Voight, James Caan (not to mention again George Hamilton!) *and* Al Pacino had all passed on the part of Ted Kramer before he'd finally accepted it. Give the man a break! So what if the first script had a few other superstar fingerprints on it? That happens all the time. The point is that, once it was rewritten, he recognized its importance. Dustin has always been a man who likes to have his life make sense both artistically and personally, and he could readily see that the theme, interaction and resolution of *Kramer vs. Kramer* would do much to help him understand himself.

What ended up on screen, though, was much more than one man's search for understanding. Instead it became an international statement for people who didn't know Ted Kramer's pain and certainly for the countless thousands who'd lived it themselves. His performance struck a unique chord in the sad song of marital disenchantment. He told one reporter that, as for having to choose one parent over another, 'It doesn't sound like something I would want to experience if I were a child. I wouldn't want to experience it as an adult, and I don't believe children are much different from adults.'

Dustin's beliefs in children seemed grounded in his own experience. True he had had only one sibling to deal with as a child (and one good-looking enough to be a movie extra, lest we forget) but he also had the brief associations of temporary schoolmates he'd bumped lunchboxes with over the Los Angeles school system as his family moved around looking for their proper niche. Those brief encounters and that lack of making real friendships from them, served, ultimately, only to underscore his loneliness. When he finally did have a family and friends of his own, he was both thankful and shy about how to handle them. Many times he resorted to a professional position.

Dustin's relationship with his cinema son, Justin Henry, showed this. 'There came a day when it was all over and we had to say goodbye. I loved that kid. I said goodbye . . . and I've never seen him since.' When he related this on *Good Morning, America* during the publicity for *Tootsie*, there were tears in his eyes that a make-up man could never duplicate. But the movie was over, the closeness that went with it was gone, and as he'd had to do so often in his own life, Dustin moved on and tried not to look back.

The present and the future were the most important, and looking back to the crazy. 'I'll do anything to survive' days at Macy's toy department, you know he'd never have taken the joke of selling Robert Duvall's son one step further than it went. He had loved his stepdaughter, Karina, from the moment he met her and continued to tell interviewers that he, one day, wanted many more children.

For a time Dustin felt that his ten-year marriage would somehow come back together, that some patient angel would smile down and mend the broken union, but it never happened. His tall and beautiful wife would not be coming back, and as that fact became clearer he could do little else but accept it. Reconciling himself to Anne's private needs, he was able to step back far enough from his own life to comment on two-career marriages: 'I'm in awe of the ones that work.'

As he questioned his failed marriage, he also questioned his career. And at that time it was understandable. Having no idea of the enormous effect that *Kramer vs. Kramer* would shortly be having on virtually every moviegoer, he said he felt empty and unfulfilled, not having accomplished anything of consequence. 'I keep feeling I haven't done anything yet.' Thankfully for him, he was shortly proved wrong.

# 14

## The elusive Oscar finally won

The reception *Kramer vs. Kramer* got, from both critics and the public, quickly brought Dustin back from what he considered a creative graveyard, for not only did it dissipate his artistic disillusionment about *Straight Tim* and *Agatha* but it also restored his screen image. With the proper material and the chance to personalize it, as he'd done with Ted Kramer, he proved he was still a most profitable star.

As for his co-star, Meryl Streep, the film proved to be the 'open sesame' to major stardom that thousands of actresses have wished for.

It was a cool New York night when she went to the official wrap party given by Benton at an Upper East Side New York watering-hole called *La Bote*. By now the triumvirate of the film, Hoffman, Benton and Jaffe, knew how potent a performance Meryl had given, but the public had yet to learn. When she slunk into the party, looking like a latter-day Garbo in casually chic clothes, the fans and papparazzi gathered in front barely noticed her as all cameras were being readied to focus on Dustin's arrival. Her camera-wise co-star, though, fooled them all by entering through a back door into the kitchen—where he stayed most of the evening, chatting with the chef. That night was probably one of the last times Meryl would go unrecognized, because the reception her performance in *Kramer vs. Kramer* was about to receive made her an international star. Benton, its director, knew it already, telling her that her talent was so enormous that 'You can literally do anthing.' Shortly, after her work in *The Deer Hunter* and *Sophie's Choice*, she would prove Benton totally correct in his enthusiastic statement.

When *Kramer vs. Kramer* opened nationwide in November 1979, reviewers and public alike quickly heralded it as *the* movie event of the year. Dustin received some of his best notices since *The Graduate* and, in fact, many saw *Kramer vs. Kramer* as almost a sequel to this earlier film. It did seem logical that Ben Braddock might easily have evolved into the lifestyle of Ted Kramer, complete with beautiful wife and child, an upwardly mobile job and a logical optimism that his life would continue in a smoothly ascending curve to ever greater success and happiness. When it all falls apart in front of his startled eyes, due to the demands and pressures of the emerging eighties (all of which were based on the moral changes of the sixties the era Ben personified) it's easy to see the connection. And just as Dustin's Ben had become an icon of his time, so would Ted Kramer come to symbolize the eighties man. Dustin wasn't particularly happy about turning into another 'generational hero', but it seemed to be his artistic fate.

When the flood of reviews and box-office tallies began coming in, no false modesty kept Dustin from acknowledging his contributions to its success—or his gratitude for being able to have done so. While everyone knew there'd been many vocal confrontations during the making of the film, 'Benton allowed me what no other director before had allowed me. He let me try to constantly do better.'

In another interview he stated, simply, 'You can't rush quality. That's the key, but most people who make movies today aren't concerned with quality. All they're concerned with is making money.' *Kramer vs. Kramer* was not only awash with quality but already on its way to be one of the biggest money-making films in history!

Benton said of Dustin, 'I found him a tireless worker, one who was constantly preparing, discussing, questioning scenes and situations. He was there every second I allowed him to be. His energy and intelligence sustained him when the rest of us were exhausted.'

Rave reviews and box-office success have a magic way of soothing any ruffled feathers, but Dustin was not soon to forget the débâcles of his two First Artists flops, *Straight Time* and *Agatha*—films in which he was specifically denied his full input. Almost gloatingly he told film-writer Wanda McDaniel, 'Art is revenge', and *Kramer vs. Kramer* handed him that in spades.

One aspect of *Kramer vs. Kramer* that the critics picked up on was the sense of ensemble playing among the actors, something that must clearly be laid at Dustin's door. To be sure, not everyone understood his stage-trained acting techniques but there's no doubt that his adherence to them helped make the film the classic it's now recognized as being.

For example, take Howard Duff. Cast as Dustin's lawyer in the custody battle, he was an actor from Hollywood's old school, a laconic personality at the best of times who'd made his name playing roughneck detectives and other gentlemen just a step away from the law in films like 1948's *Brute Force* and '50's *Shakedown*. Perhaps his most popular claim to fame was his 1956–7 television comedy series, *Mr Adams and Eve*, which co-starred him with his real-life wife, Ida Lupino.

To Duff, Hoffman was an object of unabashed awe. He told *TV Guide* that Dustin 'can be a pain, very wearying. All he does, morning, noon and night, is work. . . In *Kramer vs. Kramer* there was a scene where I'm supposed to be talking on the phone. He insisted on rigging up a live phone and being on the other end. But Dustin and I always got along fine. Maybe it's because we never socialized. I never went out drinking with him and wound up putting my arm over his shoulder and saying, "The trouble with you, Dustin, is . . ." '

Ironically, Duff's questionable advice might have been available to Dustin at a much earlier date when Duff was up for the part of Anne Bancroft's husband in *The Graduate*, but due to scheduling problems he wasn't able to take the part. Later he realized that was a major career mistake. 'It was a hell of a script. Everyone who saw it wanted in. They don't come along like that very often.' Instead of what might have been the kick-off of a bigger screen career, Duff worked consistently but in small roles as he did in one of Robert Benton's first films, *The Late Show*, made in 1976 with Lily Tomlin and Art Carney, and as an unlikely reincarnation of Sidney Greenstreet in television's lurid, and unpopular, version of the 1949 Joan Crawford movie *Flamingo Road*. Duff was a total professional, though. As such he blended in with the rest of the *Kramer* cast and, not surprisingly, turned out a fine performance. And as it would prove with almost everyone in the film, *Kramer vs. Kramer* added new lustre to his reputation.

To Dustin, the reviews were a personal vindication, and he revelled in them. Stanley Kauffmann in *the New Republic* reflected the general tenor of writers who'd closely watched him over the years when he said, 'Dustin Hoffman is back in form—a new and better form, in fact.' *New York Magazine's* David Denby went even further, saying he 'gives the most detailed, the most affecting performance of his life.'

While Meryl was on screen for less than a third of the picture (while Dustin was in almost every scene), her reviews were equally rewarding. She walked away from *Kramer vs. Kramer* with a reputation as the screen's hottest new star and, shortly, an Academy Award for Best Supporting Actress.

When the Academy nominations were announced early in 1980, *Kramer vs. Kramer* was up for a grand total of nine. Of that nine, it eventually won the most important ones. (Ironically *Agatha* slipped into the nominations too, for Costume Design—remember Redgrave's hats and furs?—but lost to *All That Jazz*.)

Just as Dustin had been continuing to learn the facts of marital life (including the sadder ones), he'd also learned a few facts about the Academy Awards. *Kramer vs. Kramer* was his fourth Best Actor nomination out of only seventeen films. Approximately one-quarter of his screen work had reached this highest echelon of approval, from *The Graduate* (1967) to *Midnight Cowboy's* tortured Ratso Rizzo, to 1974's *Lenny* and now Ted Kramer. It was an awesome tribute to his talent that could be rivalled by very few others. To him it was an opportunity for revising opinions just as life had stepped in to revise his personal options, and, instead of calling the Awards a pointless charade and 'ugly and grotesque' as well as patently unfair, he took a page out of his character Ted Kramer's diplomatic Madison Avenue approach to life and wised himself up to the commercial ways and means of Hollywood. In short, he decided to play the 'Academy Game' and agreed to a personal publicity blitz to sell him and the picture, making himself available to interviewers and reporters in a way he'd never done before. Just as Kramer was the Yuppie survivor, so did Hoffman become the upwardly mobile Yuppie movie star, and it was a startling revelation. To his credit, he spent no time denying his earlier opinions of the award process but, instead, told people for the first time about the problems he'd had to deal with over the years to get decent work on the screen. He wasn't apologizing but was stepping over the broken pieces of his past work onto fresh ground. His frankness won him many new friends and only made *Kramer vs. Kramer* an even bigger hit.

'It's not all that easy to come out of a film with something decent. The movie industry isn't exactly steeped in honour,' he candidly told *Focus on Films*. 'In fact, even when they do promise you something and put it into your contract, they find ways of finagling so you don't have what you thought you had.' (This was in obvious reference to his First Artists difficulties, a legal situation that has never been totally resolved!) Admitting he was difficult to work with and did insist on certain demands being met, he explained, 'If I'm going to spend 2½ years of my life on a project, as I did with *Kramer vs. Kramer*, then I've got to be more than another puppet actor. I need, really need, to be part of the entire creative process from start to finish.'

And when the Academy Award nominations were announced, on 25 February 1980, it all seemed finally to make sense when *Kramer* received its nine nominations.

To a large extent the ensemble aspect of the film was reflected in those nominations. Dustin's Best Actor nod reflected his overall influence as the core of the story, the suddenly single parent who, overnight, has to cope with every aspect of his and his child's life. Playing the son who causes his father many anxious moments and forces him to face readjustment, Justin Henry was nominated in the Best Supporting Actor category. Meryl's nomination as Best Supporting Actress seemed to underscore and validate her often irritating habit of improvisation to get her part right, while Jane Alexander's nomination in the same category gave credence to her role as the well-meaning friend of Joanna whose feminist beliefs Dustin immediately suspects as being at the root of his wife's desertion.

Alexander's part was small but pivotal. Ted confronts her immediately upon Joanna's leaving, accusing her of helping to cause it. Playing a divorced parent herself in the film, Alexander eventually contributes to Ted's reconciliation with his new circumstances, becoming an important friend to him while doing so. (It was Alexander's second nomination for a Hoffman film, the other being *All the President's Men*, and she's been quoted as saying that one of the main reasons she takes these small parts is because they're of such dramatic input to the story that she need never worry about ending up on the cutting-room floor during final editing!)

For blending the story and actors into a potently caring mixture, Robert Benton was nominated for both Best Director and Best Screenplay Based on Material from Another Medium while cinematographer Nestor Almendros received a nomination for his photography and Jerry Greenberg for editing it all together. The nominations proved just how well everyone had worked as an ensemble crew, a point underscored again with the nomination for Best Picture of the year.

Rivals for the 1979 Academy Awards were some of the most powerful in years. *This* was no year of filling out the categories with also-ran movies and so-so performances when there were the likes of *Apocalypse Now* and *Norma Rae* around. The Best Picture nominees, besides *Kramer vs. Kramer*, of course, were Bob Fosse's *All That Jazz* and the critically applauded youth comedy *Breaking Away*.

Up against Dustin for the Best Actor award were four other heavyweights; Jack Lemmon for *The China Syndrome*, Al Pacino (an actor briefly considered for Ted Kramer) for . . . *And Justice for All*, Roy Scheider in *All That Jazz* and Peter Sellers' unforgettable portrait of the out-of-time gentleman in *Being There*.

The Best Actress category wasn't one to worry the *Kramer* crowd, but it should be noted that it was as prestigious a list as any of the others, including, as it did, Jill Clayburgh, Sally Field's *Norma Rae*, Jane Fonda, Marsha Mason and Bette Midler for her dynamic screen debut as *The Rose*. Gigantic talents all.

Best Supporting Actor offered Melvyn Douglas as the stately powerbroker of *Being There*, Robert Duval for *Apocalypse Now*, Frederic Forrest as Midler's boyfriend in *The Rose*, Mickey Rooney in his comeback role in *The Black Stallion* and little Justin Henry, the Kramers' child.

As for Best Supporting Actress it was again a powerful line-up, with both Streep and Alexander up for *Kramer vs. Kramer* (a fact that usually cancels both performances out), Candice Bergen, who'd *finally* come into her own in *Starting Over*, Barbara Barrie for her understandably frazzled mother in *Breaking Away* and Woody Allen's protégé, Mariel Hemingway, for her work in his *Manhattan*.

In the Best Director category, Benton was up against an equally heavy crew of talents which included Francis Coppola *(Apocalypse Now)*, Bob Fosse *(All That Jazz)*, Peter Yates—Dustin's long-ago director of *John and Mary* *(Breaking Away)* and Frenchman Edouard Molinaro for the campy hit about female impersonators, *La Cage aux Folles*.

Blessed (or cursed) with such a wealth of pictures and performances made the Academy's job one of the most difficult in years, and while Dustin was talked about as a favourite, the track was filled with so many champions that the outcome was, truly, anyone's guess.

By the time of the Awards, *Kramer vs. Kramer* had grossed over $60 million at the box office, making it one of the all-time ticket-selling champs. And Dustin had been honoured with a Golden Globe Award as Best Actor of the Year. During his acceptance speech he rationalized that, 'People will forget who won this year in a very short time', after which he handed the award to producer Stanley Jaffe. With tongue only partly in cheek, he supplied a telling anecdote to the banquet when he added that, 'I also want to thank divorce.'

Next the Los Angeles Film Critics' Association jumped on board the accelerating *Kramer* bandwagon when they handed the film its award as Best Picture, Best Director to Benton, Best Actor to Dustin and Best Supporting Actress to Meryl. As the days narrowed down to Oscar time, it seemed that *Kramer vs. Kramer* was destined to be a big winner.

But tell that to Dustin! After all, this was his fourth time at bat and he was of the school that nothing—least of all anything in the film business—was worth getting excited about until your name was on the contract or, in this case, you held the golden statuette. He'd been approached by the Academy to present the most pres-tigious Life Achievement Award to Sir Alec Guiness on the Award night of 14 April 1980 and was pleased to do so. It was presented early in the invariably lengthy proceedings, and Dustin came onstage to present it to find himself amidst a chorus of cheers. Appropriately humble, he introduced Sir Alec by saying, 'I know of no other actors in the story of film who touch this man's work, and it's a great tribute to introduce him to you.' Naturally Guiness needed no real introduction but the point wasn't lost that the new generation of stars were finally, and happily, in a position to honour those who'd paved their way. 'He's what all actors strive to be,' Dustin concluded, before bowing off and letting Guiness appreciate his ovation.

The early awards were given out amidst the usual plethora of over dressed women and uncomfortably tuxedoed men. As a teaser, the show's producers had decided several years earlier to give out the supporting acting awards early in the show to keep audiences watching for the big finale, and when Meryl won Best Supporting Actress the response was wildly enthusiastic. It didn't look like a clean sweep for *Kramer*, though, when Justin lost his Best Supporting nomination to Melvyn Douglas in one of those not-so-rare tributes to a veteran who'd been overlooked during most of his career. The technical awards of Cinematography and Editing were lost to *Apocalypse Now* and *All That Jazz* respectively, but there was still lots of suspense to be gone through when Benton won the award for Best Screenplay.

That suspense and its accompanying enthusiasm shortly paid off when Benton was named Best Director, *Kramer vs. Kramer* won Best Picture—and Dustin won Best Actor. Finally it seemed that everyone agreed he deserved it, including the Las Vegas odds-makers who'd voted him favourite at 1—4, with his competition rating this way: Sellers 5–2, Pacino 3–1, Scheider 6–1 and Jack Lemmon the longshot at 15–1. Way back in 1958, when Susan Hayward finally won her Academy Award after numerous nominations, someone said: 'Hollywood can breath easy at last now that Susie's got her Oscar.' Hollywood breathed another huge sigh of relief this night when Dustin, at last, won his!

Ironically Hayward's reasons for Oscar anger was that she *wanted* to win, while Dustin didn't believe, until *Kramer*, that he really *deserved* to. Susan attended many Oscar evenings, basking in her stardom (as well she should have), but this was, after all, only the second time Dustin was there, the first being his 'innocent' year of *The Graduate*. And he didn't even want to win! 'After I got the nomination, I thought, "Ok, it's *enough* already for this one part." '

Later, when John Wayne won for *True Grit* over Dustin's work in *Midnight Cowboy*, he was delighted, feeling the award should be for an actor's body of work—'good, meritorious work—an honour, not a contest.' During the *Lenny* proceedings Dustin was hard at work on his play *All Over Town* and couldn't attend. He explained to one noisy LA news reporter who'd tracked him down that that was why he wouldn't be there, adding, however, his personal opinions about the award's commercial aspects versus its artistic integrity. The reporter didn't air the interview until Oscar night and, edited, it came out like a classic case of sour grapes. Dustin's outspoken words were heard by one of the Oscar night's hosts, Frank Sinatra, who became incensed because he felt Hoffman had put down the Academy. On stage during the show, Sinatra said that 'with all due respect to Dustin Hoffman, this is *not* an obscene ceremony', a statement Dustin was shocked to hear as he sat watching the show in his far-away hotel room. He considered himself badly misquoted—although he did say that he'd admitted he thought Oscars were 'ugly and grotesque'—and a myth became created that night that he was rabidly anti-Oscar and not deserving of any more of its attentions. Indeed it was five years before he was nominated again, but to lay that fact at Sinatra's door is patently ridiculous. The ageing crooner, then teetering in and out of singing 'retirement' and a couple of dreadful films (does anybody remember *Dirty Dingus McGee*?), certainly didn't have the power to influence any Academy members, with the possible exception of himself.

Dustin's opinions about awards in general is that they delight only the winners and 'hurt the hell out of the ones that lose'. When Dustin made that statement it was at the Golden Globes shortly before the Oscars, when his little friend and co-star, Justin, had just lost not only the Best Supporting Actor nod but the New Star of the Year award as well. Justin was in tears and Dustin was angry.

But on Oscar night Dustin was pleased at winning his Oscar. It had taken him thirteen years and seventeen films but he'd proved his point, which was, basically, leave the kid alone and he'll come through. He was now in a position to be gracious and generous and he was both of these things during his acceptance speech. He underscored that he was accepting it not only for himself but for the many hundreds of unsung actors over the years who'd dreamed of winning one but never got close. He realized that *Kramer vs. Kramer* was a touchstone film soon to set off a new trend in film-making with pictures like *Ordinary People* and *Terms of Endearment*, stories of family life in the new decade of the eighties.

And he was also happy to take home Oscar because he'd *earned* it the hard way. As he later said, 'God knows I've done enough crap in my life to grow a few flowers.'

# 15

# The past catches up

With the triumph of *Kramer vs. Kramer* behind him, Dustin was finally ready to take a long period of time off from being a movie star to become, again, just an ordinary man. Naturally the success of *Kramer* brought him many offers, primarily the film version of *The World According to Garp*. At the time, if her was tempted by anything, it would have been a suitable Broadway stage project, and with that in mind, he turned down director George Roy Hill's movie project flat. (Shortly after he did this, in late October '80, he was amused to read trade-paper items which said that Hill was scouting for 'a young Dustin Hoffman' to play Garp. Obviously Hill wasn't going to take Dustin's rejection without a snipe at the star who'd rejected him. Robin Williams ultimately played Garp, and while critics loved his interpretation, audiences were left confused. Although the film ended up being acclaimed and honoured, it was not the success that Dustin would likely have made it.)

It might well have been another benchmark film for Hoffman, but he had other things on his mind.

Just two months after his Oscar win in mid-April 1980, his mother, Lillian, suffered a major heart attack, followed within weeks by a stroke. Her younger son was distraught. Lillian was the one woman he'd always been able to count on through the thickest and thinnest of times. And suddenly he was losing her. As one friend put it, 'she was not only your biggest fan but sometimes your *only* fan.'

Backtrack to Dustin's youth. Though he'd always wanted to be closer to his family as a whole, he always remained an outsider, a stance he'd unwittingly strengthened by marrying outside his religion. He found out the hard way that, for a nice Jewish boy, a 'shiksa goddess' was not the answer. The divorce from Anne was a hardship to be accepted, endured and then forgotten. His two daughters, adopted and natural, were his only rewards, and he was very grateful for that.

Once the marriage was over and the divorce in progress, Dustin reverted to the basic values of his culture that he'd really been looking for all along. His WASP goddesses were behind him, and at forty-three he finally understood where the best kind of happiness could be found. Her name was Lisa Gottesgen.

Way back in 1967, before *The Graduate* made him a movie star, Dustin had gone back home for a small family reunion at his parents' Beverly Hills house, where they'd been living since his father's furniture-design business took off. By that point the Hoffmans had established a real identity in the neighbourhood, not to mention close friends.

Mother Lillian's best friend, Blanche Salter, lived right next door, and she was at the party with her ten-year-old granddaughter, a child Dustin had once babysat for years earlier. A classic little beauty with an un-Hollywoodized name and nose, she was as innocent as any Beverly Hills child could be, and she was very happy re-meeting the neighbour's son, aged thirty. He hardly noticed the little girl, but she noticed him!

Many years later he joked to *Good Housekeeping* that, 'It's not incest, but it's probably only one step removed because I played "doctor" with Lisa's mother when we were six years old. The day I met Lisa again I was an unemployed New York actor playing piano at this party, and this little girl in pajamas sat next to me. Later, when I walked away, she turned to her grandmother and said "Nanny, I hope he waits for me, 'cause I'm going to marry him when I grow up!" '

Eight years later they met again at another family party. By then Dustin was a major star of thirty-seven while she was just eighteen. Also, by then, 1975, he was happily married and Lisa was getting ready for college, where she wanted to study law. Dustin was quite taken with her youthful, quiet beauty and shy manner and offered her a job as an assistant in helping to keep his LA affairs in order what with his constant running between coasts. Her grandmother, Lillian's best friend, supervised the budding friendship and occasional meetings to make sure it was all very innocent.

Obviously, though, Dustin was attracted to Lisa, and when his marriage broke up they became closer friends, slowly building on their feelings and heritage which had been present all these years. 'I fought it,' he admitted. 'The relationship with Lisa was born out of resistance in a sense because I didn't want my first marriage to end. I didn't get married to Anne until I was thirty-one, and I thought that by holding off so long I had a good shot [at making it a success].' To many, a decade-long marriage was a good shot indeed, but once it was over Dustin was gun-shy all over again.

Happily, Lisa exhibited a rare and unquestioning patience while Dustin handled his emotional devils. The divorce from Anne had left some open sores but she was ready to let them heal. In a candid comment about Hollywood marriages Dustin remarked, 'I hear about divorced people who remain friends but it kinda makes you suspicious, doesn't it? Very Noel Coward, I think,' and, to his mind, just about as believable.

Lisa was also a young woman who was showing signs of practicality, self-reward *and* the space blithely to forget it all if she wanted to. While working long and determinedly on getting her law degree from UCLA, she thought of it only as a back-up to her real goal in life. Said Dustin in a candid moment, 'Her desire is to have kids.' Or, in other words, to have a basically husband-wife relationship. Dustin, bombarded with nubile stars and starlets, recognized this honesty and thought all the better of Lisa for it.

The difference in their ages became common knowledge after reporters began spotting them in public—after all, the difference between the woman he was leaving and the woman who was taking her place was papparazzi news—but he was still unable to discuss the relationship except to take a protective stance for both their sakes. 'She's my attorney—and if you're not careful, I'll have her sue you.'

Also, after his years with his much-taller first wife, Dustin seemed to feel much more at home and more protective towards Lisa—'Lisela', as he calls her.

As for her, with her un-made-up face and naturally curly hair, she seemed to revel in his protectiveness, if not, particularly, in his success as a superstar. She seemed the kind of girl who'd have stood by him if he gave up the movie star life on a moment's notice, without ever looking back! The closer they became, the more honest she was in her feelings that whatever life he chose, where he went, she would also go.

By the time his mother became so seriously ill, they were in love, only waiting for his final divorce papers before they'd wed.

When they visited Lillian after her stroke, both were devastated to find that it had paralysed her entire right side, leaving her unable to speak. *Rolling Stone Magazine* chronicled Dustin's desperation as he rushed into her room at LA's Scripps Memorial Hospital, his hair wildly amess after the helicopter ride that got him there. Lillian was in bad shape. She was dying, although no one wanted to admit it. Emergency surgery was suddenly scheduled and all the Hoffmans knew just how immediately necessary it was.

Dustin grabbed the arms of his father and brother Ron and pulled them down close enough to Lillian's face to show her that the Hoffman family was together again. They'd never been so close before, and they'd never be that close again. All past acrimonious thoughts and feelings didn't matter anymore. Mom was dying, and, if there was ever a moment to be a family, it was now.

This crisis opened their eyes and, while she couldn't openly express it, there must have been a happy light in Lillian's eyes as well.

'This is a tough one, Mom,' Dustin later said. 'You really *got* to fight.' Turning quickly from his father to his brother, he kissed them both. 'Did you see that Mom?' he asked her, almost begging for a positive reply. There was a slight wink of acknowledgement from Lillian which came just before they took her off to the operating room. Turning to Lisa, he looked to the future. 'We've got to have a baby. We've got to give my mother a reason to live.'

Four months later on 12 October 1980, just a few days after his divorce from Anne became official, Lisa, twenty-five, and Dustin, forty-three were married, and after a quick honeymoon in Hawaii they almost immediately announced her pregnancy. Lillian lived another year, long enough to see the baby, Jacob, born in March 1981, and know her wayward and often headstrong son was firmly back in the family.

Lisa had graduated from UCLA Law School in June '80, and her wedding to Dustin a few months later was a quiet one, 'an intimate garden ceremony with only about eighteen close relatives, friends and a rabbi'. Since Lillian was unable to attend, Dustin tried making her feel a part of it by bringing a rabbi to her hospital room where he performed a traditional Jewish betrothal ceremony for the bride and groom-to-be at her bedside. Due to her long friendship with Lisa's grandmother, Lillian considered her immediately as part of the family, and happily Dustin's two daughters accepted her without reservation. But to Dustin, after her long years of concern over his life and happiness, it was essential that his mother knew how fulfilled he felt now. He never doubted it again, when, after the betrothal ceremony, she gave another tiny wink of approval.

Dustin's new life almost came to a swiftly tragic end when Lisa nearly died giving birth to their son. It was early in March and she was in her eight month of pregnancy when her abdomen suddenly became hard and she began losing consciousness when she lay on her back. There should have been bleeding to warn them of the seriousness of the condition but the placenta was ripping away from the uterine wall and stopping the blood's flow. Unknown to them, if the placenta continued tearing away, the resultant internal haemmorhaging would kill Lisa and the lack of oxygen would also kill the baby.

Dustin somehow sensed the seriousness, despite the doctor's somewhat blasé reaction of just bringing Lisa to the hospital to be checked out. Putting her in the car, he sped to Santa Monica Hospital, where doctors in the emergency room immediately assessed the seriousness of her condition. They decided she needed an immediate Caesarean section. Dustin wouldn't leave Lisa and stood in a corner of the operating-room in quiet shock, watching while the doctors cut open his wife and took out their baby. The doctor said, 'He told me later it blew his mind that a twenty-nine-year-old woman was telling him what to do, was operating on his wife and saving his baby. He learned that there are things in life completely out of his control.'

Later Dustin was to learn that, had Lisa gone unattended, she'd have been dead within the hour. It was a sobering experience and one he'd never forget, lightened only by the happy fact of a healthy wife and a baby boy they immediately nicknamed Jake.

Naturally the touch-and-go events leading up to Jake's birth were kept from Lillian, as she needed as much peace of mind as possible. During her last year, though, she must also have had some other happy moments with the emergence of another woman in her family, a lady named Dorothy Michaels, alias *Tootsie*. Dustin was working on that project during her final months and frankly admits that she was his inspriration.

'Every time I felt physically uncomfortable during the shooting of the picture, like when the wig itched or the shoes pinched, I'd put on a happy face for my mother's sake. I told her I was doing the film before she died and she was very proud. She *was* my inspiration.' Had she lived to see the results, Lillian Hoffman, the gay and spunky blonde who'd once practised to be a movie producer's glamorous consort, would have been mightily proud.

'Dorothy has her strength, her vulnerability, her vitality and sexual humour,' Dustin said later. 'My mother had the spirit of a chorusgirl. At seventy-two she was still playing two sets of tennis a day; she had Ann Miller's legs.'

125

Dustin's brother, Ron, a Washington DC economist, felt that *Tootsie's* Dorothy Michaels was vitally important to him because the character 'was keeping her alive while playing that part'.

Certainly if *Tootsie's* Dorothy Michaels reflected *one-tenth* of Lillian's vivacity and spirit for living, Dustin was successful in his long-lasting quest for perfection over the long months it took to make the film. With her inspiration to guide him, plus the input of his own ideas and those of friends, he managed to create a character so special and so unique that it deserved all the rewards that it would shortly enjoy.

# 16

## *Tootsie* is created

Dustin's lifelong avocation of learning and knowing women evolved from Lillian to Anne, to Kate Jackson, to Lisa and even to Joanna, his screen wife in *Kramer vs. Kramer*. It was only natural, then, that there would come a day when he asked the ultimate question of himself. What if *I* were a woman in today's society? For Dustin it was a logical progression of the kind of thoughtful self-questioning he constantly indulged in as an actor. And it was a matter much on his mind. The boy who'd been snared by Mrs Robinson was now a man dealing with real life. The death of his mother, his divorce and remarriage and the subtle questions raised in *Kramer vs. Kramer* all led him to look for an answer.

It was also logical that he should turn to one of his oldest and closest friends, Murray Schisgal, to help him in his quest. After *Kramer*, Schisgal asked Dustin point-blank what he'd like to do next—and Dustin told him, 'Let's see if I could play a man forced to impersonate a woman, then experiencing life from the other point of view.'

It *was* an intriguing idea, especially with Dustin Hoffman as the star of such a project. Here was the symbol of the rebellious sixties male in *The Graduate* who'd turned himself immdiately into a social outlaw in *Midnight Cowboy* and, after that, into the sole survivor of Custer's Last Stand in *Little Big Man* and then into Lenny Bruce, the ground-breakingly foul-mouthed comic in *Lenny* and, eventually, helping break open the Watergate conspiracy in *All the President's Men*. If that wasn't enough, he had changed into the embodiment of the alienated, workaholic husband, Ted Kramer— and now he wanted to change himself into a woman? Talk about an actor coming full circle! For openers, would anyone believe it?

As the idea became more firmly implanted in his mind, Dustin knew he wanted to do new things with it. This idea would not end up as a remake of *Some Like It Hot*, in which Tony Curtis and Jack Lemmon had impersonated women on the run from gangsters.

127

Instead, he was determined to make it a story of survival—a man's survival as a woman.

According to *The Films of Dustin Hoffman* by Douglas Brode, the germ of Dorothy Michaels came from a script called *Why Would I Lie?*, 'about an out-of-work actor, whose agent says, "You want a part in a soap opera? Only problem is, the character's a woman." I liked that, so I took the skeleton of the idea and sent it to Schisgal to develop.'

The pair batted ideas and roughly developed pages of dialogue back and forth for months, trying to devise a believable storyline. What eventually evolved was deceptively simple: an out-of-work actor poses as a woman to get a job. There, however, the simplicity ends and the fun begins.

The character of Michael Dorsey was based loosely on Dustin himself and his early years in new York when he was fired from parts and was, in short, often considered to be a temperamental pain in the neck. Anyway, the character is so intense that he lost one job in a commercial playing a tomato because he argued with the director about a tomato's ability to sit down! Finally his agent tells him he's unemployable, at which point Michael decides to prove him wrong.

As a favour to his girl-friend, Sandy, Michael coaches her for an audition for the role of the administrator of mythical Southwest General Hospital—television's favourite soap opera. Sandy doesn't get the part but Michael decides to try for it, getting himself up as a woman, storming into the audition and winning the role! At first it's a marvellous challenge as he stretches his character, making her more and more forceful, to the point where Dorothy Michaels, his assumed female name, is suddenly one of the most famous and beloved 'women' on television.

By this time Michael/Dorothy has fallen in love with one of his co-stars on the soap, the beautiful nurse Julie—'I'm the hospital slut,' she cheerily introduces herself—and befriends her. She returns his affection as a girl to girl and takes him to her father's farm for a weekend holiday where her *father*, Les, proceeds to fall for him as Dorothy.

Now Michael/Dorothy is truly up against it but his character is so popular that there's no way he can get off *Southwest General*. Meanwhile Sandy intercepts a box of candy from Les to Dorothy (whom she still knows only as Michael) and thinks he's gay. When he tries to express his true feelings to Julie (who only knows him as Dorothy), she thinks he's a lesbian!

It's sidesplitting slapstick comedy as Michael/Dorothy tries to juggle his various identities and relationships and find a solution. The opportunity comes when one day the show has to go on the air live because of a technical foul-up. Improvising wildly, Dorothy/Michael unmasks himself in a wildly implausible yet hilarious monologue. Along with millions of viewers across the country, Sandy is watching the show, as is Les, and they both react in sheer horror at his unwilling deception. His room-mate, Jeff, is also watching but he just shakes his head in resignation, commenting 'This is weird stuff.' At the end of the story Michael and Julie get together with special insights into each other's character that, hopefully, will make their relationship stronger.

To make the whole thing work, though, was the utter believability of Dustin as Dorothy Michaels, and getting her down right took over a year's work. Dustin was to be paid a staggering $4½ million salary plus a percentage of the profits to make Dorothy come to life and he devoted himself to the project with his usual total immersion and dedication.

Much later, as part of Columbia's extensive promotion of the film, *The Making of Tootsie* hit television screens, and it gave great insight into how Dustin, literally, became Dorothy.

Some of the most fascinating scenes, obviously filmed during production, were of Dustin in the make-up chair scanning pasted-up photos of Marilyn Monroe while Monroe's make-up guru, George Masters, worked on turning Dustin Hoffman into Dorothy Michaels. In even more painstaking detail than we see in the film itself, Dustin's face undergoes an awesome change under Masters' expertise in a time-consuming process that, eventually, was boiled down from 3½ hours per day to about two.

Despite Masters' genius, there was one problem that couldn't totally be concealed and that was Dustin's heavy beard, his five o'clock shadow as it were. Every morning at home, 'I take a sauna shave—as close as you can get,' but after the hours of having the elaborate make-up applied there was not much time left for shooting scenes before his beard's shadow would begin to show through, making him look like a man in drag. There was nothing to be done for it and whenever Dustin sensed that he wasn't looking totally right, he'd be compelled to stop working, feeling he couldn't photograph as he was supposed to. By now his attachment to Dorothy Michaels had reached an obsessive point, and he *refused* to compromise her. Because of that, many very expensive production hours were lost.

129

Masters' make-up was extraordinary, starting with a thick foundation he developed which worked to smooth out the skin totally, filling in Dustin's teenage acne scars which now are almost gone but which could be glimpsed in the harsh close-up lenses of the cameras. Another Masters invention, small tabs of adhesives attached in front of the ear and then drawn back by elastic bands, drew back any jowly skin, leaving a clean chin line, was only one of many tricks in his magical make-up bag. Masters wiped out Dustin's face, leaving a blank canvas on which to create the persona of Miss Dorothy Michaels. Using all his skills and a counter full of assorted cosmetics and eyelash-curlers, he does an incredible job, and, as Masters works on the exterior we can see Dustin/Dorothy working on the inner woman, letting his voice rise to Dorothy's light, Southern-lilted falsetto and then carrying on a conversation with Masters in that voice, using, stretching and teasing it to a point where he could submerge his masculinity into Dorothy's femininity. The finishing touch was added when an overlay of false teeth was superimposed over Dustin's rather ferret-like ones to create a more feminine, glisteningly perfect smile.

Dustin's said there was a 'constant creative war going on over the interpretation of Dorothy', yet much of it was waged within himself. Once the make-up was set—after months of trial and error—Dustin was disappointed that Dorothy wasn't prettier. 'I wanted her to be. She deserved it,' he says. 'Once I saw that I was never going to be really pretty, it was painful. It hit me when I realized that I wouldn't take myself out or go to bed with me.' Ironically that personal reaction sparked Dustin to wonder what he might have missed growing up, since Dorothy was exactly the kind of woman he'd never been attracted to himself in reality.

Dorothy gave Dustin a chance to explore the female psyche in a way he'd always wanted to. After *Kramer vs. Kramer*, he felt there was still much to be said about the contemporary woman, and *Tootsie* gave him a chance to probe and explore the question.

'After a year, when the day came when I looked and sounded like a woman, then I made a crucial decision,' Dustin told *American Film Magazine*. 'I'm not going to try to do a character; I'm just going to be myself behind this and see what happens. And that's what I did. I had to assume a southern voice because it held my voice up [in range].'

Many people helped in creating Dorothy Michaels besides Dustin and Masters, including Larry Gelbart, the official screenplay-writer, Schisgal, Elaine May, on board as a writer for a while who's credited with introducing Bill Murray's room-mate character into the proceedings, who proved to be a brilliantly comic counterpoint to Michael's ever-growing intensity, and Polly Holliday.

Dustin and Polly had remained friends after *All the President's Men*, and he turned to her now to help him perfect his southern accent. She happily agreed and they spent hours reading *A Streetcar Named Desire* aloud—with Dustin playing Blanche! Holliday, a perfectionist much in Hoffman's mould, gave him his last lesson and ultimate compliment when, without looking at him, she listened to his accent and was convinced she was hearing another woman.

Once the make-up, the dress style and the sound of Dorothy Michaels had been established to everyone's satisfaction, nothing would do but that Dustin test it out in public. Just prior to the start of production in April, he ventured into the streets of New York to explore how it felt walking them as a woman.

*En route*, he found out a thing or two about what a woman *shouldn't* do to be attractive. The late Arthur Bell of New York's *Village Voice* newspaper cheerfully related one particular incident. Dustin/Dorothy was in an elevator with a friend when who should walk in just as the doors closed for the downward trip but José Ferrer. The friend introduced Dorothy Michaels to the noted actor, at which point Dustin whispered in his Dorothy-voice, 'Oh Mr Ferrer, ah loved you as that little man in *Moulin Rouge*. How'd ya like to have your cock sucked?' Ferrer, aghast, waited until the elevator hit the bottom floor and the doors opened before replying to the friend, 'Who is that scumbag broad?' Later Dustin chortled, 'I fooled Toulouse Lautrec!'

Reportedly he also fooled an old co-star, Jon Voight, at New York's Russian Tea Room (used in the film as the first place where Michael as Dorothy confronts his agent with his new identity). It's certainly understandable that the *Midnight Cowboy* would not recognize Ratso Rizzo in drag.

Shortly afterwards Dustin visited his daughter Jenna's school, asking to be introduced to her teacher, a woman he'd met occasionally over two years. He arrived from the *Tootsie* set in full regalia during the school's lunch hour, and his embarrassed daughter begged, 'Daddy, please get out of here,' but Daddy persisted: 'Just introduce me as your Aunt Dorothy from Arkansas,' which Jenna proceeded to do. 'And you know,' Dustin

131

recalled later, 'that teacher treated me differently from before. There is a kind of sisterhood among women,' he told *People* magazine. 'I never got that before. Women are wary with men.'

When filming began, on 1st April, at the recently refurbished Astoria Studios in Queens, the site of many silent film classics and later to gain renewed fame as the studio where the super-costly *Cotton Club* was filmed, director Sydney Pollack had corraled a magnificent cast of actors, including Charles Durning as Les, Bill Murray as Michael's zany room-mate, Teri Garr as Sandy, the delightful George Gaynes as the ageing Lothario actor on *Southwest General*, Dabney Coleman as the soap's chauvinistic director, Ron, and Pollack himself stepping in to play Michael's agent. Said Pollack of his casting himself, 'Dustin kept begging me to do it, sending me flowers, so I finally said OK, feeling that, if I did that for him, he'd lighten up on a few of his demands.'

As Dustin got deeper into his character, this 'little picture' started turning rapidly into a mammothly expensive one. (By the time shooting was completed, on 3 August, the original budget of $10 million had more than doubled, to $22 million.) Unfortunately, at this time there had been several monumental box-office flops in Hollywood which had actually undermined studios, not to mention the careers of their stars. One was a $40 million Western, *Heaven's Gate*, and another was a product of the same studio financing *Tootsie*, Columbia, the $50 million musical *Annie*, directed by John Huston. (Why anyone in their right mind would pick action-director Huston for such a project is beyond me— and just about everyone else for that matter. It's akin to Brian De Palma directing *Splash* or Woody Allen making *Body Heat*!) In any case, as *Tootsie's* budget expanded, the rumour-mills began referring to it as 'Hoffman's Folly', speculating that it would never be successful.

But Dustin just ignored the stories as he was much more interested in getting the film right, which included locating just the right person to play the beauteous nurse, Julie.

After working with Meryl Streep in *Kramer*, he was anxious to continue a professional association with the new young breed of actresses who were redefining the term 'movie queen' in the eighties. He realized that these women harked back to the forties when strong female personalities such as Joan Crawford, Barbara Stanwyck, Roz Russell and Ann Sheridan dominated the screen with bravura performances. They'd all but disappeared by the fifties, with lightweight newcomers such as Janet Leigh, Debra

Paget, Terry Moore, Doris Day and Elizabeth Taylor (before she learned how to screech!) taking over as sweet young things who were usually cast opposite ageing male stars who'd retained their box-office power. Just as Dustin had spawned a new breed of leading man with *The Graduate* in 1967, so had these women forged a renewed female screen image in the late seventies and early eighties. Sally Field, Sissy Spacek, Jane Alexander, Dyan Cannon, Julie Christie and Faye Dunaway were all prime examples of this new feminine screen power, as was his soon-to-be Julie, Jessica Lange.

After her screen debut in 1976's laughable remake of *King Kong*, the former covergirl seemed a most unlikely prospect to join these ranks, but after her critical success in Bob Fosse's *All That Jazz* and the steamy remake of *The Postman Always Rings Twice*, Hollywood (read 'casting directors') began looking at her in a new and brighter light.

When word started getting out about the riveting work Jessica was doing as the tragic film star Frances Farmer, in *Frances*, even the hardest-nosed critics began smiling. When she finally finished *Frances*, she was physically and emotionally exhausted, having been deeply affected by her role as the traumatized actress. Kim Stanley, the great character actress who played *Frances'* crazily domineering mother, advised her to 'do a comedy', and, only three weeks after finishing *Frances*, she decided to take her advice. 'I almost said "no" to *Tootsie* because I just couldn't imagine having the energy after *Frances*.' Happily, she found it and, in doing so, shortly found herself up for two Academy Awards —one for Best Actress (*Frances*) and one for Best Supporting Actress (*Tootsie*). Talk about an actress, for once, listening to some good advice!

Jessica's stamina paid off, and she also found herself in a position to learn a few lessons that would come in handy later, when she became one of the producers of *Country*, primarily that of being able to differentiate between simply acting and acting with a hand in the overall production decisions. It wasn't something she necessarily wanted to learn, but exposed to it she certainly was. 'I never sensed that the producer's job was to be the captain of the ship. My sense is that the director has that job . . . I simply cannot split myself into different people when I am acting,' she said at the time. 'On *Tootsie* I one day realized how truly different Dustin is from me. Dustin could one moment by playing his character and the next moment be dealing with Sydney

133

Pollack and the following moment be dealing with the wigs. I'm totally different, and if that means I am aloof, so be it. But there's a reason. I am not, by nature, a performer. Some people are, by nature, performers.'

If there must be a parallel drawn, it would seem that, at that time, with Lange's intensity as an actress still relatively new to films, and still inwardly smarting from the stings of *King Kong*, she could not envision herself trading one hat as star to the other as producer so she simply divorced herself from that aspect of the business and learned her lines. For Dustin, though, it was another story. His fifteen years in the business and seventeen films precluded that because he'd learned the hard way that, to get what he wanted on screen, he'd have to fight for it.

And fight he did, over every line and detail, but the rushes were beginning to look much better, and the mounting rumours that it was a doomed project were ignored. One undeniable reason for the evergrowing budget was, as usual, Dustin's perfectionism. Many times he'd gladly do a scene Pollack's way but only if, in return, he got to do it again as he saw it.

It was all part of an arrangement the pair had hammered out when Pollack initially told Dustin that the only way he'd direct *Tootsie* would be to be its producer as well, territory Dustin had stamped out for himself. 'But you're taking away all the controls I've earned over the years I worked on the project,' Dustin shot back. Pollack wouldn't budge, so Dustin gave in, 'But even that was with an agreement that I would get script and cast approval . . . and be able to disagree and even show alternatives.' In all some 500,000 feet of film was shot, often showing some of those alternatives—of which only 10,000 would wind up on the screen.

Wisely Columbia Pictures found a way to use some of the footage when, in March 1983, its fifty-minute documentary, *The Making of Tootsie*, was offered to more than a thousand media outlets covering all the commercial bases from regular syndication to public television to pay-television networks, touting it as a 'behind-the-scenes'look at a major film in production. The film, according to its Press release, 'contains actual footage intercut with conversations with Jessica Lange, Teri Garr, Bill Murray, Dustin and director Sydney Pollack.'

While the documentary was a good idea and very interesting to watch, *Tootsie* hardly needed any more publicity by then. Since its Christmas opening it had quickly become the biggest box-office hit in the country, particularly in New York City, where it had been filmed. For months those city-dwellers had had a front row seat as Dustin made Dorothy Michaels a reality. And Lisa was always there on the set for moral support, often with their baby son. Said Dustin, 'I've been doing this since he was eight weeks old. He thinks going to work means putting on a dress. Luckily we can afford therapy for him later.'

The Hoffmans had set up housekeeping in Manhattan's old but swanky San Remo apartments, again near Central Park where Dustin often went jogging. The place set him back over $1 million and was actually two apartments with the walls between removed for extra space. Slowly he and Lisa poured another $2 million into the renovation and furnishings, giving Dustin a chance to educate her in his hobby of collecting antiques. Lisa made sure that it was a constant refuge from his on-the-set conflicts. And, in short order, she became pregnant again.

Once the film was wrapped in August and then went into the editing rooms, word of mouth began building about what an extraordinary film was about to be unleashed on the public. Though its budget had topped out at $22 million, Columbia's executives began breathing easier, even to forgetting their qualms that *Tootsie's* star had been off the screen since *Kramer vs. Kramer* almost three years before.

As he'd done then for that film, Dustin opened himself up to the Press for a marathon of interviews all primed to sell *Tootsie* to the world. One event that got a lot of coverage came ten days before the film's official premiere, when the New York Branch of Women in Film announced him as an honorary member. He was delighted and told the women he'd happily play a female again 'if, the make-up wasn't so hard'. Wisely he omitted his chance encounter with José Ferrer as he reeled off several more anecdotes.

Advance reviews were so good that Columbia decided to launch the film in the grand manner, and on 16 December 1982 Mann's Chinese Theatre in Hollywood was packed with stars prepared to welcome *Tootsie*. On their way in through the celebrated crowd, both Dustin and Lisa looked nervous (especially Dustin when cameras were around) but Lisa, in a dark dress with a Peter Pan collar, at least managed a smile.

Shortly into the film, when Dustin first appears as Dorothy walking down a crowded Fifth Avenue, the audience exploded in laughter, and it didn't let up until the end. So enthusiastic were they that several people commented they wanted to come back and see it again because they'd missed dialogue because of the uproar.

At the nearby Brown Derby restaurant, everyone was in a mood to celebrate, descending on the film's stars *en masse*. Besides Dustin, Jessica Lange, Teri Garr, Charles Durning and Sydney Pollack were all on hand. Pollack was with his daughter, Rachel, while Lange was without her *Frances* co-star and constant companion, Sam Shephard. She spent most of the evening with Durning, both accepting praise from such people as Jackie Bisset and Alexander Gudonov, Peter Falk and his wife Shera, and Valerie Perrine, Dustin's old *Lenny* co-star, who was on the arm of *Love at First Bite* director Stan Dragoti.

Pollack was also deluged with praise over his performance from virtually everyone, one notable exception being actress Doris Roberts who told him, 'The role should have gone to an actor, there are too many actors out of work.' Obviously Doris didn't know the details surrounding Pollack's deal with Dustin, and, besides, Sydney had never really warmed to the idea of playing the agent anyway—'It's too difficult being split in two like that'—but, he added, 'You know Dusty. If he wants something, he'll find a way of getting it.'

Even Barbra Streisand was lured out of hiding by *Tootsie*, along with Shelly Duvall, Christopher Reeve, Tina Turner, Tatum O'Neal and Michael Douglas. The superstar word-of-mouth got *Tootsie* off and running that night but, naturally, Dustin's biggest regret was that his mother couldn't have been alive to share in the fun. After all, the title of the movie came directly from her, because when he was a little boy she'd call Dustin her 'little tootaie'. Now *Tootsie* belonged to the world, and was the world happy to meet her!

# 17

# Living happily with success

As had happened with *Kramer vs. Kramer*, *Tootsie* immediately became the must-see movie of the year, and Dorothy Michael's name was on everyone's lips. It exploded into 1983 with sensational word of mouth that shot it to the top of the box-office charts to the number-one position—where it stayed for some thirteen weeks. In Hollywood, New York City and even Oshkosh, if you hadn't run right out to see it you were either in Intensive Care or visiting a Third World country. It was a phenomenon that was impossible to ignore.

*People* magazine called it a 'giddy, glorious surprise' and, while noting the contributions of Lange, Durning, Garr etc, stated '*Tootsie* belongs to Hoffman, who gives it a triumphant freshness that is at once funny, elating and emotionally satisfying.'

The Hollywood Reporter's Robert Osborne drew out seldom-used adjectives (especially by him!), calling the film 'the quintessential Christmas gift, a film that will not only spread undiluted Yule joy . . . but also has the qualities to ultimately lay in as an enduring comedy classic'. Osborne briefly underestimated Dustin's interpretation by comparing it with other men-in-drag movies such as Jack Benny's *Charley's Aunt* and the Curtis-Lemmon-Monroe classic *Some Like It Hot*. Those men were in women's clothes to escape aspects of life, where Dustin's Dorothy put on a dress to *live* it to a fuller potential. Osborne was totally on-target, later in his review, when he said that, 'The plotting could hardly be better, with every scene and situation making a point, and keeping *Tootsie* on a constant chart of amusing suprises.' He called the ensemble acting 'flawless' and said that Dustin was 'feisty, determined and vastly amusing'.

Much attention was paid to George Masters' exceptional make-up wonders in transforming Our Hero into Our Heroine, and also deserved praise came Jessica Lange's way as the woman of Michael/Dorothy's dreams to whom he can't express himself without giving his own game away. Reviewers were quick to pounce on her heretofore unknown comic abilities (especially in light of her concurrently running *Frances*). Ironically she'd shown a portion of these talents just before in *How to Beat the High Cost of Living*, with Jane Curtin and Susan St. James, but it, and fewer still remembered it. Yet, as the dipsy soap-opera star, Julie, she won extraordinary reviews and renewed appreciation. *King Kong* was long gone in this, her banner year.

Bill Murray preferred to let his role leap out at the audience without any title billing, and the suprise and humour of his Jeff earned him a great deal of critical applause. The *Saturday Night Live* veteran contributed a subtle, off-the-wall counterpoint to Michael's madness in juggling his identities. Teri Garr was singled out for critical attention also.

In fact, when the Academy Awards nominations were announced, *Tootsie* raked up ten of them! It was nominated for Best Picture, Best Director to Pollack, Best Actor to Dustin, Best Supporting nods to Lange and Garr, Best Screenplay Based on Material from Another Medium, Best Cinematography, Best Film Editing, Best Original Song and, finally, Best Sound. It was a crackling well-earned list, and Columbia, pleased not only by the nominations but by the phenomenal box-office the film was doing, decided to join the yearly trade-paper Oscar campaign with a series of full-page ads pointing up *Tootsie's* finer points.

When other awards began pouring in, there were more ads to point it all up to the Academy. *Tootsie* was on a roll that seemed unstoppable. It took Golden Globe honours as Best Picture, Best Actor to Dustin and Best Supporting Actress to Jessica. The National Society of Film Critics gave it those same three awards plus Best Screenplay, while the distinguished New York Film Critics heralded Pollack as Best Director, Lange as Best Supporting Actress and the film, again, as Best Screenplay.

Between award announcements the ads continued using snippets of important reviews, calling the screenplay, credited to Larry Gelbart and Murray Schisgal, 'a model of comic construction' (*Variety*), with praises of its 'hard ball dialogue . . . it has an exquisite balance and central core' (the *LA Times*).

Reviews for Pollack were also outstanding, with attention given to the fact that he 'registers a double whammy . . . by virtue of his beautifully sustained direction as well as his vastly amusing supporting performance as Hoffman's agent' (*Variety*).

All the reviews and hoopla were enormously gratifying to Dustin, and it showed. He and Lisa had been welcomed in '83 in London, where he was promoting the picture. Very obviously pregnant, Lisa was smiling and happy in a high-collared dark dress. Dustin was happy to pose for photographers, putting his hand on Lisa's stomach, exclaiming, 'The only thing I want for 1983 is a nice healthy, bouncing baby for us.'

The photographers found Dustin relaxing with his wife, Michael Caine and David Bailey at Langan's Brasserie, a smart club of which Caine was a co-owner. A little after midnight the Hoffmans took a break from the party by stepping out onto the street for some fresh air where the obviously delighted and carefree star stood for about forty-five minutes, even shaking hands with many fans who happened by and recognized him.

Ironically Columbia didn't take out any full-page ads after the nominations came out, for the simple reason that Dustin towered so over the project that he was impossible to ignore. Jessica found herself in a rare position when she also received an Academy nomination as Best Actress for *Frances* but that didn't tarnish Columbia's enthusiasm for her *Tootsie* performance and full-paged her using quotes such as David Ansen's from *Newsweek* which said how 'she brings a beguiling spacy sensuality, Monroe-like in its poignancy to her part.'

In all, 1983 was turning into a banner year for Dustin. He won another Best Actor nod, this time on the televised special *Your Choice For The Film Awards*. The night he was due to accept, Dustin was in bed with the flu and a 103-degree temperature but, realizing that the award was a public tribute—coming from the moviegoers themselves—he got out of his sickbed and attended. After receiving his trophy from Cloris Leachman, he was even able to manage a quiet quip about how hard it had been getting used to high-heeled shoes and then ended by thanking the cast and crew of *Tootsie* 'for holding that lady up'.

Meanwhile Tootsie-mania continued sweeping the country. Even the mayor of Houston, Texas, Kathy Whitmire, got in on the act when her constituents couldn't help but notice the incredible resemblance between herself and Dorothy Michaels. She was quoted as saying that she was 'amused at the whole thing', and it certainly didn't hurt Houston's *Tootsie* box office. Dustin as Dorothy sent Her Honour an autographed photo.

And George Masters found a mini-career travelling around the country making up local talk-show hosts into hometown *Tootsies*, carefully shaving eyebrows and then using his amazing talents with varying degrees of success.

The emotional highpoint of the year for Dustin came on 20 March when he got his New Year's wish, a baby daughter. The Press gossiped that if the baby was a boy it would be named Hamlet, Hercules, Max or Zack and if a girl Diana, Vanessa, Agatha (an unlikely choice) or—Dorothy. The happy couple settled on the classical Rebecca.

Movie offers poured in in the wake of *Tootsie's* success, and Dustin almost had the lead in *Gorky Park* but the producers would not match his huge previous salary. In March it was reported that he was seeking out director Taylor Hackford (*An Officer and a Gentleman*) for a project called *The Glory Boys*, but so far nothing has come of that.

The following month it was rumoured that Mike Nichols wanted Dustin to reprise his Carl Bernstein role in *Heartburn*, based on the semi-documentary novel by Nora Ephron, Bernstein's by-then ex-wife.

He said no to *Blade Runner* too, and his old Broadway mentor, Zev Bufman, was interested in having him for a revival of *Inherit the Wind*.

One project that Dustin was reportedly very interested in doing was a comedy with Blake Edwards, *The Man Who Loved Women*. The volatile pair even started preliminary work on a script before Edwards did a complete turn-around and cast Burt Reynolds instead. Dustin was reportedly incensed over the incident and accused Edwards of using one of his ideas in the film. Said Dustin, 'All Reynolds has to do is wink at the camera and he's a star—I'm short and ugly and really have to act.' It might have made an interesting film with Dustin in the lead but with Reynolds it turned into a major flop, maiming Edwards' career and practically killing off Burt's!

Oscar night proved disappointing for the *Tootsie* crowd, however, as only Jessica Lange walked away a winner as Best Supporting Actress. Ironically, as had happened with Meryl Streep in *Kramer vs. Kramer*, she won her award for a part that at second glance seems equally as important as Dustin's. Her character helped his make sense.

It took a while, almost a year in fact, but Dustin did win an award for *Tootsie*—or, at least, half a one! On Sunday 25 1984 the British Academy of Film and Television Arts named him and

Michael Caine (for *Educating Rita*) as Best Actors of the year. Dustin was delighted, happy that the picture continued proving itself to audiences around the world. He celebrated in his own quiet way by purchasing a painting by the late Milton Avery for $108,000 for his new home. Then he thoughtfully sent Avery's widow an invitation to visit and see how he'd displayed it.

Money-wise he could easily afford the purchase as *Tootsie's* international figures were closing in on $200 million, $95,197,000 of which was in the United States and Canada alone. An extra benefit was the expanding video-cassette marketplace where, by then, a staggering hundred thousand tapes had been sold for home viewing machines at $79.95 each!

Salary and profits from *Kramer vs Kramer* and *Tootsie* made Dustin enormously rich, and his days of *having* to take on a part were finally over. He was rich in another way, too, and that was in his new understanding of women. He's admitted that Dorothy Michaels has been the most difficult character he's played to leave behind, most likely because of its close connection with his late mother. One of the greatest self-realizations that Dorothy brought him came when, during the developing of the character, he realized that she was too old to bear children. 'I think it's a little late for that,'he said in his Dorothy whisper, and completely broke down in tears.

'I still miss her,' he says, and in fact kept Dorothy's wardrobe in four huge wardrobe trunks in his LA office. Lisa wanted some of them, as did her grandmother, Blanche, and Jane Fonda approached him about donating some to a charity auction. Dustin refused them all, but Lisa isn't worried.'Why should I be? So far he's not trying them on.'

Another side-effect of his playing Dorothy has been to make Dustin a more tolerant person—'at least my wife thinks so. Lisa says that now when I take the wrong turn on the freeway or spill something, I just shrug it off like Dorothy instead of banging on things and cursing as I usually do.'

Movie producers kept cajoling Dustin with offers, the most interesting of which was a sequel to *Chinatown* to be called *Two Jakes* in which, hopefully, for a reported salary of $5 million, Dustin would take his place alongside Marlon Brando, Jane Fonda and Jack Nicholson, who would be reprising his Jake Giddes character from the original film.

But Dustin was tired, and that project also never got past the talking stage. Instead he and Lisa spent much time with their children at their house in Roxbury, Connecticut, a house complete with a swimming-pool and tennis court. It was a time of getting back to normal for him, although that did not mean a time of mindlessness. Dustin had always hated so-called vacations because he becomes swiftly bored with nothing to do. 'I need a vacation to recover from a vacation,' he once said, and that was true. Often he enjoys shopping with Lisa for her clothes although his basic uniform—of blue jeans accented by some old piece of a movie costume he's kept—has remained unchanged. And despite his substantial wealth, they were never designer jeans! As for the costume pieces, it wasn't just Dorothy Michael's clothes he'd saved but bits from all his films which, when worn, brought back memories and were, well, practical. He always has been, and remains, a practical man who learned the value of a dollar the hard way and has never forgotten the lesson.

Summer in Connecticut is about as beautiful an environment as one can find, and Dustin enjoyed it fully. He'd go out jogging in the sparkling mornings and often wave at neighbours as he padded by doing his usual four to eight miles a day. 'If I'm feeling old, I only run four.' One of his neighbours in Roxbury, who he'd often toss off a wave to, was playwright Arthur Miller, who lived nearby in the same house where he'd married and briefly lived with Marilyn Monroe.

Running had always given Dustin time to think, and he shortly began thinking about what he'd like to do next, finally deciding that he wanted to return to the Broadway stage—actually a place he'd truly yet to conquer. In the back of his mind was the idea of doing the play he'd always dreamed of—Miller's *Death of a Salesman*. The only problem was that Dustin didn't feel he was old enough yet, at forty-seven, to carry it off. Broadway's orginal Willy Loman, the main character of the story, had been played by Lee J. Cobb at the age of thirty seven and when Dustin let this sink in, he decided that, at the very least, it was something to talk about. Who better to talk to than the master writer himself, who lived just down the road?

A surprised Sally Field and a delighted Dustin backstage after just
having received their Academy Awards as Best Actress and Best
Actor of 1979. Hollywood could breathe easier now – Dustin finally
had his Oscar!

Time out for Dustin and director Sydney Pollack on the hectic New York City set of *Tootsie*. The film provided a months-long free-for-all for the New York tabloids which played up every disagreement between the star and the director

Can this *really* be my client Michael Dorsey (Dustin Hoffman)? ponders his agent, George Fields (Sydney Pollack) in *Tootsie*

City girl, Dorothy Michaels (Dustin Hoffman), shares a bucolic moment with Les (Charles Durning) in *Tootsie*

*Tootsie* struts her stuff!

'Michael Dorsey' responds to a joke on the often-troubled set of *Tootsie*. The production went weeks over schedule and many millions over budget but once the public got a look at the results it all proved eminently worthwhile. Dustin's dual role as Michael Dorsey/Dorothy Michaels should have earned him a second Oscar

Accepting the 'Your Choice For The Film Awards' rather bulky trophy from Cloris Leachman as Best Actor of 1982 for *Tootsie*, Dustin left a sick bed with a 103 degree fever to be there. In his acceptance speech, he graciously thanked the cast and crew for 'holding that lady up'

# 18

## Death of a Salesman

In June '83, Dustin visited Miller at his home and mentioned to him his desire to go back to the stage. According to Mel Gussow of the New York Times, an old friend of Dustin's, his host's first reaction to this was, 'You don't want to do Salesman, do you?' What thrilling words to hear from the author himself, but he still feared it was too soon in his career.

It had been almost twenty years since the afternoon when Ulu Grosbard took time away from directing *A View From the Bridge* to point out his stage manager, Dustin, to his friend Miller, telling him that he was an actor who should one day play Willy Loman. Ironcally, when the time came when Dustin was cautiously considering doing so, Grosbard was long gone from his life. But Arthur Miller had remembered his words.

Dustin and Miller had several meetings about *Salesman* during which Dustin became increasingly encouraged, especially when Miller offered to restore some original dialogue which referred to Willy Loman's shortness, only a few lines but so pertinent that they would subsequently become a touchstone of Dustin's performance. With such total co-operation from Miller—a man whose talents Dustin vastly respected—he decided to undertake the role that he'd secretly been longing to play for so many years. The closest he'd ever come to it was when he had a small part in a recorded version of the play which had starred the original Willy, the late Lee J. Cobb.

Since Dustin had now reached a position of total independence, he insisted that he have approval of cast and director as well as supervising his own make-up which would transform him into a failed, road-weary, sixty-three-year-old salesman. Talk about a quantum leap from *Tootsie*!

The first major step he took towards finding his Willy came when, after trying and rejecting a series of wigs, he agreed to have his head virtually shaved to accommodate a thinning hairpiece.

He also decided to change his body size. 'I'm going to lose weight. I want to be just skin and bones. Willy has been trying to kill himself for six months [figuratively]. The play is the last twenty-four hours of his life.'

Dustin approached his Willy Loman with his sense of almost neurotic perfectionism, submerging his own personality into that of the failed salesman who'd never been able to capture his share of the American dream even though he always tried facing life 'riding on a mile and a shoeshine'.

Just as Dustin's mother had been his inspiration for Dorothy Michaels, it was his father, Harry who gave him his first insight into Willy Loman. Now in his late seventies and living in La Costa, California Harry had had hurly-burly years during the thirties and forties, and his attendant disillusions were much like Willy's with his constant search for success and not being able to find it. 'My first anchor for Willy was my father,' said the actor, who later elaborated that a little bit of Arthur Miller got in there too.

Joining with Robert Whitehead, Roger L. Stevens and Miller as a co-producer under his Punch Productions banner, the star agreed to a minimal salary of $735 a week until (hopefully) the show went into the black, after which he'd receive a percentage of the gross receipts. Director Michael Rudman was signed on and the casting began. Over a period of four months, Miller, Dustin and Rudman auditioned five hundred actors for the play's thirteen available roles.

Wearing a makeshift costume with a vest and a battered forties hat he found on Columbus Avenue in a thrift shop (and which he took to wearing all the time to disguise his shaved head), Dustin found that while auditioning actors he could also learn and explore the play and its relationships even more. 'It was like free rehearsal time,' he said. For the part of Willy's successful next-door neighbour, he originally wanted his old friend Gene Hackman, but Gene, though intrigued by the idea, had film commitments. When it came to casting Willy's larcenous brother, Ben, Dustin had the quirky inspiration to call in Watergate burglar G. Gordon Liddy for a reading, but the part eventually went to an old acting friend of Dustin's Louis Zorich. Kate Reid was cast as Willy's wife, and a multitude of young ladies—including a former and the current wives of Norman Mailer—were considered for various other female roles.

His friend Bob Duvall suggested that for Willy's son, Biff, Dustin should check out a young actor named John Malkovich who was then playing in *True West*, the Sam Shephard hit play. Malkovich, though, was then being tempted with a movie offer, *Places in the Heart*, and took that instead of signing a potentially long run-of-the-play contract. Dustin's second choice was a major suprise—Robert De Niro.

Hoffman and De Niro on the same stage was an inexhaustibly exciting idea but, said De Niro, 'You want me to play your *son?*' Dustin persuaded him at least to come down to the audition hall, which he did, looking around, talking ideas and then commenting on how Dustin, in vest and battered hat, was already getting into his character. Dustin told Gussow his reaction to that comment: 'It was like a fighter coming in to see another fighter, and saying, "I see you're using a left hook and so on "' Doubtful that it would have worked, Dustin simply postponed the whole project until Malkovich finished his movie (for which he was later nominated for an Academy Award, no less!) and signed to play Biff.

Once the cast was completed, rehearsals began amid much enthusiasm. Miller was quoted as saying that Dustin was going to produce an entire new persona for Willy unlike anything done before. 'He's a cocky little guy overwhelmed by the size of the world and trying to climb up to the top of the mountain. Dustin will create a new Willy . . . It'll be his Willy.'

Unfortunately, when the play went on the road for try-outs, stopping first in Chicago, that 'new Willy' had yet to materialize. *Variety* spent most of its review praising Malkovich while calling Dustin 'problematic in the central role. His Willy Loman lacks the buried streak of nobility that makes his fall tragic. He is a sixty-three year-old man who shuffles from place to place although he has no known history of ill health. It's obvious that Hoffman has prepared the role intensively . . . But his own persona—street-smart and alley-wise—often gets in the way.'

The *Chicago Sun-Times'* Glenna Syse thought that the forty-six-year-old actor's transformation into a haggard sixty-three-year-old salesman was almost *too* convincing. 'Underneath the old crow, we have to have hints of the young bantam rooster. Before this show goes to Broadway, I would suggest [they] throw out Stanislavski and go back to the streets.'

Other critics noted that the audiences 'did not seem knocked out' by the production, although the *Chicago Tribune's* Richard Christiansen wrote positively that Dustin 'genuinely seems to have been an old-line salesman working the New England territory for the last thirty years.' As usual with Dustin, the critics couldn't have been harder on him than he was on himself. During a small gathering after one performance a reporter called to him as he was leaving, 'I'll call you next week,' to which he replied, 'I may be at Forest Lawn,' the famous Hollywood cemetery.

About the only solidly good news Dustin got during that January run came when Lisa told him she was expecting their third child.

Luckily there was still time to work on the play before Broadway critics could sharpen their teeth on it when the company moved on to Washington, DC. One way Dustin tried tightening the performance was by exchanging acting notes between himself and the actors who played his sons Malkovich and Stephen Lang. They even did this during the intermission of the performances, an experience Dustin likened to seeing movie rushes and then being able to re-shoot (in this case re-play) the scene more effectively the next day. Malkovich was frankly awed at Dustin's obsessive quest for constant improvement. 'He is as relentless a performer as I've ever encountered. He will never give up on a single moment in the play until he thinks it's perfect, and I don't think he'll ever think it's perfect. A lot of stars cast mediocre people around them and put them in a dim light, but he wants everybody around him to be very good.'

Between work and performances in Washington, Dustin found the time to take Lisa and the kids to visit the National Air and Space Museum at the Smithsonian Institution for an outing. Despite the increasing pressures as the play got closer to Broadway—he felt 'cautious'about it—his family came first, always providing him with the safety of uncritical people who loved and appreciated him for himself.

By the time of the Broadway opening night at the Broadhurst Theatre on 1 April, Dustin was still feeling 'cautious' but also optimistic as well. He felt he was giving the play his best shot, and nobody can do more than that—not even Dustin Hoffman.

As it turned out, the revival of *Death of a Salesman* took New York by storm, and critics raved about Dustin's 'bold' and 'unique' Willy Loman. They even recognized and lauded the small dialogue changes Miller had made for him, especially in the pivotal scene where Willy's searching for a reason he's not liked. 'I'm short,' he moans, instead of 'I'm ugly', which had been Lee J. Cobb's line years before. The Hollywood Reporter seemed to sum up opinion when it proclaimed Dustin's work 'a tragic, yet somehow joyous, portrait.' Miller's disconsolate drama of the ageing salesman whose life and family fall down around him shortly became the season's hottest ticket, with all doubts of Dustin's ability to carry it off swept away in a rush of ticket sales. Sure there might have been people coming in hopes of seeing *The Graduate* or the *Marathon Man* but they walked away with respect for yet another new facet of Dustin's seemingly limitless talent.

A major disappointment came when he wasn't nominated for a Tony award, but the committee considered the play a revival and therefore ineligible. The same fate befell his co-stars, Reid and Malkovich, as well as Al Pacino, who had also blasted Broadway that year in a revival of *American Buffalo*. Many of the Broadway commentators argued not only that Dustin should have been nominated but that he should have won as well.

At the end of April producer Robert Whitehead looked at the projected box-office figures and tried to persuade Dustin to extend the play's run beyond its 10 June cut-off date. Dustin thought about it and told Whitehead he'd be agreeable if he could cut out one of his eight performances per week, pleading the strenuosity of the role left him exhausted. The producer agreed to that, but the matter caused *New York Times* critic Walter Kerr to quip that, 'People who earlier suggested the actor was too young to play Willy Loman [are] now beginning to wonder if he mightn't be too old.' It made for a funny remark, but no one who'd seen Dustin on stage could really take it seriously.

At the age of forty-eight he may well be just coming into his own—as he's always privately seen it. After the incredible success of both *Kramer vs. Kramer* and *Tootsie* (his profits from the latter film are estimated at some $21 million as of this writing!), he's in the enviable position of being able to call whatever shots he wants. His success has made him a member of an elite group of stars including Burt Reynolds, Clint Eastwood, Harrison Ford and Richard Gere, a club that operates from choice.

And what might those be? Dustin has mentioned projects from time to time that he'd like to tackle on screen. With tongue in cheek he's mentioned doing the life of Harpo Marx, citing 'The main reason I want to do it is to keep leaping after the girls and squeezing that horn.' In a more serious vein he's mentioned others. 'There are many characters that still intrigue me,' he wrote a few years back. 'Hitler has always been an enigma and a challenge to me. And I would like to do a film on the Hollywood political climate of the 1950s . . . Dalton Trumbo [the blacklisted screenwriter] would be a great character to centre on.' Also the lifestory of flamboyant Broadway producer Jed Harris has been proposed to him.

Whatever the choices might be remains to be seen, but Dustin's inherent disbelief in his own charisma will likely be a part of them. 'You still have to look forward to the worst which will come maybe with the next review, when it will finally be revealed to all, including yourself, that you are a fraud.'

Yet, as much as reviews are important to the success of a film or play, they've never influenced Dustin's career decisions. And for a very simple reason. As he's said, the only thing that truly matters is how an artist personally feels about his work, and Dustin's work, next to his wife and new family, has always been the most important thing in his life. Looking back at disappointments like *Alfredo, Alfredo, Agatha* and *Straight Time*, he's quick to point out that, often, 'You see your own work and you know yourself what's good and what's bad. You know where you could go back and improve it and you wish you could.'

Always the perfectionist, he's never forgiven the producers who've put out his less-than-best work and, more importantly, he's never forgiven himself for letting it happen. So adamant is he now on retaining control of his project that 'The "book" on me is that I can turn a go project into a development deal.'

Yet despite Dustin's public image as an often surly and silent star, he's earned a quiet reputation as a giver, though seldom to public causes. What he gives, he gives alone, not for any printed payback but as a personal return for the success he's achieved. As a young man he worked in Harlem as an acting-coach/director to underprivileged kids. Much later he met youngsters much like those he'd once worked with who wanted to start a recreation hall as a local gathering place. He gave them one, complete with a swimming-pool and a basketball court. The children he'd taught had helped him have a rare opportunity of artistic expression, and he was more than willing to pay the next generation back.

During the traumatic hospitalization of his mother, word leaked back that an elderly woman patient wanted desperately to meet him. Tearing himself away from his mother's bedside, he spent several hours with her, 'holding her hand and making her laugh'.

Tales abound about his private generosity but they are not stories Dustin particularly wants told. When he can help someone in real need, he simply goes ahead and does it, using the same forthright persistence that he's used on movie sets to get the job done.

148

And there's nothing more likely to tap his heart than an underprivileged or handicapped child. No doubt this stems from his own unhappy childhood looks and the joyful condition of his new family today. He's a grateful man, and a giving one. And as a happy husband and father, he's only too glad to assist the less fortunate. Not exactly *National Enquirer* news but just the plain truth. As one person said, he helps others 'not for publicity . . . He does it because he feels it's the right thing to do.'

Recently he went public for a cause but only because he felt that by doing so he could waken others to help as well. When a cousin of Lisa's, Pepper Abrams, needed help to start a camp for children afflicted with cancer (as was her own child), he stepped forward to help, calling in celebrity friends like Neil Diamond, Michael Jackson, Richard Chamberlain, David Soul, O.J. Simpson and Christopher Atkins to get involved. The group shortly got support from MacDonald's hamburger chain and today there exists a Camp Ronald MacDonald for Good Times in Southern California where these ill children can go. He appeared on *Good Morning, America* to help publicize the need for public donations, saying, 'There's something about being a part of a cause that's revolutionary. Cancer is being cured for the first time in history, and this whole new community of people are living with it and are going to be living with it, and no one can under-estimate the therapeutic value of a place like this to *help* them live with it.'

As time goes on for Dustin, some problems have just seemed to resolve themselves. For years, both publicly and in the eyes of several casting directors, he was constantly being confused with Al Pacino. When this has happened in public, the only thing that calms him down is knowing that the same thing constantly happens to Pacino as well.

Then there came a day when they were both in a famous Fifth Avenue bookstore in New York having a quiet chat among the bestsellers. (As artists, there's a lot of mutual respect between them and always has been.) Anyway, one bedazzled customer saw them, rushed over and demanded to know, 'Which of you is which?' Pacino said he was Hoffman, Hoffman said he was Pacino, and after a few scrawled lines on the woman's paperback, she left happy while they shared a good laugh.

Another problem, or rather preoccupation, that maturity—and Lisa—has solved is his ready interest in sex, which had always been a constant in his life. To writer Bertil Unger he explained that he was getting over that. 'There used to be a time when it was impossible for me to have a woman friend if we weren't lovers . . . But that seems to be changing the last few years. It's taking a while, but at least now I have some friends who are women, who are very attractive, whom I do not sleep with—but it's because they're married to friends of mine.' That was a 1980 statement, true and believable in light of his then-new relationship with his bride-to-be, yet there's still a streak of Hoffman that decries, 'Living a sexual life is the road to health.' Since his remarriage he's obviously never been healthier.

And as for his obsession with death, he seems to have that one solved too. When he has to go, he says, he wants to do it with the style of actor Jack Burns. Burns suffered a fatal heart attack in the middle of a performance and fell dead on the stage. Since he was a comedian, his fall got a laugh, 'the perfect exit.'

Dustin was in Los Angeles to be with Lisa for the birth of their third child and while there attended the closing ceremonies of the Summer Olympics of 1984. Television cameras dotted the venerable LA Coliseum, and one suddenly panned to Dustin, catching him off guard and grinning happily at the parade of international atheletes. Hair still cropped short for *'Salesman'*, he was deeply tanned and looked much younger than forty-eight, younger and more enthusiastic than the public ever sees, obviously proud of the gold medals his country's teams had won. For a man who'd gone for Hollywood Gold so many times—finally winning it on his fourth try with *Kramer vs. Kramer*—he obviously knew and understood both the struggles and the sense of constant dedication it took to be among the rare recognized winners. As the flags and athletes of 140 nations paraded before his eyes, one sensed a relaxation, a mutual recognition of excellence. In the brief glimpse the camera offered, one could sense that he, at last, felt at home among the winners of the world—and knew his own place among them was assured. The actor and the man seemed to be finally reconciled.

# Dustin Hoffman Filmography

*The Tiger Makes Out*, a Columbia Pictures Presentation, 1967
*Director:* Arthur Hiller
*Producer:* George Justin
*Screenplay:* Murray Schisgal, adapted from his one-act play, *The Tiger*
*Director of Photography:* Arthur J. Ornitz ASC
*Film Editor:* Robert C. Jones
*Music:* composed and conducted by Milton (Shorty) Jones
Running time, 94 minutes

| | |
|---|---|
| Ben | Eli Wallach |
| Gloria | Anne Jackson |
| Jerry | Bob Dishy |
| Leo | John Hawkins |
| Mrs Kelly | Ruth White |
| Mr Kelly | Roland Wood |
| Beverly | Rae Allen |
| Miss Lane | Sudie Bond |
| Mr Ratner | Jack Burns |
| Pawnbroker | Jack Fletcher |
| Mrs Ratner | Bibi Osterwald |
| Registrar | Charles Nelson Reilly |
| Receptionist | Elizabeth Wilson |
| Hap | Dustin Hoffman |
| Pete Copolla | James Luisi |

A contemporary comedy peopled with some of Broadway's most pungent character actors, *The Tiger Makes Out* found only a limited movie audience during its short term of major release to theatres.

*The Graduate*, an Embassy Pictures release, 1967
Director: Mike Nichols
*Producer:* Lawrence Turman
*Screenplay:* Calder Willingham and Buck Henry, based on the novel of the same name by Charles Webb.
*Director of Photography:* Robert Surtees ASC
Film Editor: Sam O'Steen

*Music:* Dave Grusin, with songs by Paul Simon and sung by Simon and Garfunkel
Running time, 105 minutes

| | |
|---|---|
| Mrs Robinson | Anne Bancroft |
| Benjamin Braddock | Dustin Hoffman |
| Elaine Robinson | Katherine Ross |
| Mr Braddock | William Daniels |
| Mrs Braddock | Elizabeth Wilson |
| Room Clerk | Buck Henry |
| Carl Smith | Brian Avery |
| Mr Maguire | Walter Brooke |
| Mr McLeery | Norman Fell |
| Mrs Singleton | Alice Ghostley |
| Desk Clerk | Buck Henry |
| Miss de Witt | Marion Lorne |

One of the landmark films of the sixties (as well as one of the most popular), this sensational romantic comedy broke new moral ground and made an 'instant' world celebrity of Dustin Hoffman.

*Midnight Cowboy*, United Artists Presentation, 1969
*Director:* John Schlesinger
*Producer:* Jerome Hellman
*Screenplay:* Waldo Salt based on the novel by James Leo Herlihy
*Director of Photography:* Adam Holender ASC
*Film Editor:* Hugh A. Robertson
Running time, 113 minutes

| | |
|---|---|
| Ratzo Rizzo | Dustin Hoffman |
| Joe Buck | Jon Voight |
| Cass | Sylvia Miles |
| Mr O'Daniel | John McGiver |
| Shirley | Brenda Vaccaro |
| Towny | Barnard Hughes |
| Sally Buck | Ruth White |
| Gretal | Viva |

*Cowboy* is the Technicolour odyssey of Ratzo Rizzo and Joe Buck, two of life's smalltime losers who cling to each other when the world turns completely against them. The openly expressed gay theme of the New York-set film brought homosexuality out of the closet and onto the movie screen as never before.

*Madigan's Millions*, an American-Internation Pictures release, 1969
*Director:* Stanley Prager
*Producer:* Sidney Pink
*Screenplay:* James Henaghan and J. L. Bayonas
*Director of Photography:* Manolo Rojas ASC

*Film Editor:* Antonio Ramirez
*Music:* G. Gregory Segura
Running time, 76 minutes

| | |
|---|---|
| Jason Fister | Dustin Hoffman |
| Mike Madigan | Elsa Martinelli |
| Lieutenant | Gustovo Roju |
| Burke | Fernando Hilbeck |

A slapdash Italian-made comedy, this film was made in 1967 with a low budget and rampantly disorganized script. Released briefly after the enormous success of *The Graduate*, it is now seldom seen.

*John and Mary*, 20th Century-Fox, 1969
*Director:* Peter Yates
*Producer:* Ben Kadish
*Screenplay:* John Mortimer, based on the novel by Mervyn Jones
*Director of Photography:* Gayne Rescher ASC
*Film Editor·* Frank P. Keller
*Music:* Quincy Jones
Running time, 92 minutes

| | |
|---|---|
| John | Dustin Hoffman |
| Mary | Mia Farrow |
| James | Michael Tolan |
| Ruth | Sunny Griffin |
| Ernest | Stanley Beck |
| Hilary | Tyne Daly |
| Jane | Alix Elias |
| Fran | Julie Garfield |
| Dean | Marvin Letcherman |
| Mags Eliot | Marian Mercer |

Even the presence of Hoffman and Mia Farrow could not make this tepid comedy about love and sex sixties-style work. Hoping for the success of an updated *Pillow Talk*-type film, the script—and the stars—just weren't funny.

*Little Big Man*, a National General Pictures release, 1970
*Director:* Arthur Penn
*Producer:* Stuart Miller
*Screenplay:* Calder Willingham, based on the novel by Thomas Berger
*Director of Photography:* Harry Stradling Jr., ASC
*Film Editor:* Dede Allen
*Music:* John Hammond
Running time, 147 minutes

| | |
|---|---|
| Jack Crabb | Dustin Hoffman |
| Mrs Pendrake | Faye Dunaway |
| Allardyce T. Merriwether | Martin Balsam |

| | |
|---|---|
| General George Custer | Richard Mulligan |
| Old Lodge Skins | Chief Dan George |
| Wild Bill Hickock | Jeff Corey |
| Sunshine | Amy Eccles |
| Olga | Kelly Jean Peters |
| Caroline | Carole Androsky |
| Little Horse | Robert Little Star |
| Younger Bear | Cal Bellini |

Long but ultimately fascinating study of the 'last survivor' of Custer's Last Stand, a 121-year-old man whose life provides the background for the intricate and finely tuned plot.

*Who Is Harry Kellerman and Why Is He Saying Those Terrible Things About Me?*, a National General Pictures Release, 1971
*Director-Producer:* Ulu Grosbard
*Producer and Screenplay:* Herb Gardner
*Associate Producer:* Fred C. Caruso
*Director of Photography:* Victor J. Kemper ASC
*Film Editor:* Barry Malkin
*Music:* Shel Silverstein
Running time, 108 minutes

| | |
|---|---|
| Georgie Soloway | Dustin Hoffman |
| Allison Densmore | Barbara Harris |
| Dr Moses | Jack Warden |
| Leon | David Burns |
| Irwin | Dom De Luise |
| Margot | Betty Walker |
| Gloria | Rose Gregorio |
| Sid | Gabriel Dell |
| Susan | Amy Levitt |
| Marty | Joe Sicari |
| Sally | Candy Azzara |

A misfired comedy about a rock 'n roll star and his problems gaining and then handling his success. Hoffman manages to portray believably a character who ages from seventeen to twenty-five to forty. Co-star Barbara Harris is a whacky delight in a rare film role.

*Straw Dogs*, distributed by Cinerama Releasing, 1972
*Director:* Sam Peckinpah
*Producer:* David Melnick
*Screenplay:* Sam Peckinpah and David Zelag Goodman, based on Gordon Williams' novel *The Siege at Trencher's Farm*
*Director of Photography:* John Coquillon ASC
*Film Editors:* Paul Davies, Roger Spottinswoode and Tony Lawson
*Music:* Jerry Fielding

Running time, 113 minutes

| | |
|---|---|
| David | Dustin Hoffman |
| Amy | Susan George |
| Tom Hedden | Peter Vaughan |
| Major Scott | T.P. KcKenna |
| Venner | Del Henney |
| Scutt | Ken Hutchinson |
| Reverend Hood | Colin Welland |
| Cawsey | Jim Norton |
| Janice | Sally Thomsett |
| Riddaway | Donald Webster |
| Bobby Hedden | Len Jones |
| Bertie Hedden | Michael Mandel |
| John Niles | Peter Arne |
| Harry Ware | Robert Keegan |
| Mrs Hedden | Jane Brown |
| Emma Hedden | Chloe Franks |

*Papillon*, an Alled Artists Release, 1973
*Director:* Franklin J. Schaffner
*Producers:* Robert Dorfmann and Franklin J. Schaffner
*Executive Producer:* Ted Richmond
*Screenplay:* Dalton Trumbo and Lorenzo Semply Jr., based on the novel by
Henri Charrière
*Director of Photography:* Fred Koenekamp ASC
*Film Editor:* Robert Swink
*Music:* Jerry Goldsmith
Running time, 150 minutes

| | |
|---|---|
| Papillon | Steve McQueen |
| Louis Dega | Dustin Hoffman |
| Indian Chief | Victor Jory |
| Julot | Don Gordon |
| Toussaint | Anthony Zerbe |
| Maturette | Robert Deman |
| Clusiot | Woodrow Parfrey |
| Lariot | Bill Mumy |
| Dr Chutal | George Coulouris |
| Zoraima | Ratna Assan |
| Warden Barrot | William Smithers |
| Pascal | Val Avery |
| Antonio | Gregory Sierra |
| Sergeant | Victor Tayback |
| Guard | Mills Watson |
| Mother Superior | Barbara Morrison |

# Hoffman vs. Hoffman

| | |
|---|---|
| Madame Dega | Anne Hoffman |
| Commandant | Dalton Trumbo (billed as 'Jack Denbo') |

Vital and exciting rendering of the classic novel about life behind the 'bars' of Devil's Island in the twenties. McQueen is the one who finally escapes like a butterfly. A long but ultimately satisfying film.

*Alfredo, Alfredo*, a Paramount Pictures release, 1973
*Director:* Pietro Germi
*Producer:* Not credited
*Screenplay:* Leo Benvenuti, Piero de Bernardi, Tullio Pinelli and Pietro Germi
*Director of Photography:* Aiace Parolin
*Film Editor:* Sergio Montanari
*Music:* Carol Rustichelli
Running time, 100 minutes

| | |
|---|---|
| Alfredo | Dustin Hoffman |
| Mariarosa | Stefania Sandrelli |
| Carolina | Carla Gravina |
| Carolina's Mother | Clara Colosino |
| Carolina's Father | Daniele Patella |
| Mariarosa's Mother | Danika La Loggia |
| Mariarosa's Father | Saro Urzi |
| Alfredo's Father | Luigi Baghetti |

Produced and set in contemporary Italy. Alfredo is a bewildered and henpecked young husband whose growing dream is divorce from his 'dream wife'. A social satire that misses the bullseye.

*Lenny*, a United Artists release, 1974
*Director:* Bob Fosse
*Producer:* Marvin Worth
*Executive producer:* David V. Picker
*Screenplay:* Julian Barry based on his play
*Director of Photography:* Bruce Surtees ASC
*Film Editor:* Alan Helm
Running time, 112 minutes

| | |
|---|---|
| Lenny Bruce | Dustin Hoffman |
| Honey | Valerie Perrine |
| Sally Marr | Jan Miner |
| Artie Silver | Stanley Beck |
| Sherman Hart | Gary Morton |
| Aunt Mema | Rashel Novikoff |

A blisteringly realistic biography of Lenny Bruce Hoffman plays the tragic part with believable, if uncomfortable, sincerity. Despite its black-and-white intensity, it was a huge, if unexpected, hit.

*All the President's Men*, a Warner Brothers release, 1976
*Director:* Alan J. Pakula
*Producer:* Walter Coblenz
*Screenplay:* William Goldman based on the book by Carl Bernstein and Bob
        Woodward
*Director of Photography:* Gordon Willis ASC
*Film Editor:* Robert L. Wolfe
*Music:* Davis Shire
Running time, 135 minutes

| | |
|---|---|
| Carl Bernstein | Dustin Hoffman |
| Bob Woodward | Robert Redford |
| Harry Rosenfeld | Jack Warden |
| Howard Simmons | Martin Balsam |
| 'Deep Throat' | Hal Holbrook |
| Ben Bradlee | Jason Robards |
| Bookeeper | Jane Alexander |
| Debbie Sloan | Meredith Baxter |
| Dardis | Ned Beatty |
| Hugh Sloan Jr. | Stephen Collins |

The famous team of investigative reporters, Carl Bernstein and Bob
Woodward, are brought to life in a drama chronicling their Watergate
investigation which ended in the toppling of an American president.

*Marathon Man*, distributed by Paramount Pictures, 1976
*Director:* John Schlesinger
*Producers:* Robert Evans, Sidney Beckerman
*Screenplay:* William Goldman, based on his novel of the same name
*Director of Photography:* Conrad Hall ASC
*Film Editor:* Jim Clark
*Music:* Michael Small
Running time, 125 minutes

| | |
|---|---|
| Babe Levy | Dustin Hoffman |
| Szell | Laurence Olivier |
| Doc Levy | Roy Scheider |
| Janeway | William Devane |
| Elsa | Marthe Keller |
| Professor | Fritz Weaver |
| Karl | Richard Bright |
| Erhard | Marc Lawrence |
| Mr Levy | Allen Joseph |

A taut pschycological thriller with Dustin pitted against a former Nazi for a
package of plundered diamonds. Intricate plot twists and well-realized
performances helped make this an enduring hit.

*Straight Time,* distributed by Warner Brothers, 1978
*Director:* Ulu Grosbard
*Producer:* Stanley Beck, Tim Zinnemann
*Screenplay:* Alvin Sargent, Edward Bunker, Jeffrey Boam
*Director of Photography:* Owen Roizman
*Film Editors:* Sam O'Steen, Randy Roberts
*Music:* David Shire
Running time, 114 minutes

| | |
|---|---|
| Max Dembo | Dustin Hoffman |
| Jenny Mercer | Theresa Russell |
| Jerry Schue | Harry Dean Stanton |
| Willy Darren | Gary Busey |
| Earl Frank | M. Emmet Walsh |
| Manny | Sandy Baron |
| Selma Darren | Kathy Bates |
| Mickey | Edward Bunker |

The muddled story of an ex-convict trying to readjust to the 'straight' life, *Straight Time* offers a compelling star performance somewhat hindered by erratic editing.

*Agatha,* a Warner Brothers release, 1979
*Director:* Michael Apted
*Producers:* Jarvis Astaire, Gabrik Losey
*Screenplay:* Kathleen Tynan and Arthur Hopcraft based on Tynan's novel
*Director of Photography:* Victorio Storaro
*Music:* Johnny Mandel
Running time, 98 minutes

| | |
|---|---|
| Wally Stanton | Dustin Hoffman |
| Agatha Christie | Vanessa Redgrave |
| Archie Christie | Timothy Dalton |
| Evelyn | Helen Morse |
| William Collins | Tony Britton |
| Kenward | Timothy West |
| Nancy Neele | Celia Gregory |
| Lord Brackenbury | Alan Badel |
| John Foster | Paul Brooke |
| Charlotte Fisher | Carolyn Pickles |

Interesting and ambitious account of Agatha Christie's disappearance in December 1926, fictionalized into an elegant mystery. Beautifully filmed in Britain. Vanessa Redgrave steals the picture.

*Kramer vs. Kramer,* a Columbia Pictures release, 1979
*Director:* Robert Benton
*Producer:* Stanley R. Jaffe
*Screenplay:* Robert Benton, based on the novel by Avery Corman

*Filmography*

*Director of Photography:* Nestor Almendros ASC
*Film Editor:* Jerry Greenberg
*Music:* Henry Purcell
Running time, 105 minutes

| | |
|---|---|
| Ted Kramer | Dustin Hoffman |
| Joanna Kramer | Meryl Streep |
| Margaret Phelps | Jane Alexander |
| Billy Kramer | Justin Henry |
| John Shaunessy | Howard Duff |
| Jim O'Connor | George Coe |
| Phyllis Bernard | JoBeth Williams |
| Gressen | Bill Moor |

A handsomely produced and beautifully acted comedy-drama of a man and his young son facing life alone after the departure of his selfish wife. Hugely successful and deservedly so.

*Tootsie*, a Columbia Pictures release, 1982
*Director:* Sydney Pollack
*Producers:* Sydney Pollack and Dick Richards
*Screenplay:* Larry Gelbart and Murray Schisgal
*Director of Photography:* Owen Roizman ASC
*Film Editors:* Fredric Steinkamp and William Steinkamp
*Music:* Dave Grusin
Running time, 100 minutes

| | |
|---|---|
| Michael Dorsey/ | |
| Dorothy Michaels | Dustin Hoffman |
| Julie | Jessica Lange |
| Sandy | Teri Garr |
| Ron | Dabney Coleman |
| Les | Charles Durning |
| Jeff | Bill Murray (uncredited) |
| George Fields | Sydney Pollack |
| John Van Horn | George Gaynes |
| April | Geena Davis |

An outrageously—heavily awarded—comedy about an out-of-work actor who can find work only by masquerading as a woman. The premise and the subsequent problems make for hilarious entertainment.

# Index

# Index